# Trojan War

How the Greeks Won the Trojan War

*(The History and Legacy of the Mythical Legends About the Battle for Troy)*

**Thomas Melton**

Published By **Cathy Nedrow**

# Thomas Melton

All Rights Reserved

*Trojan War: How the Greeks Won the Trojan War
(The History and Legacy of the Mythical Legends
About the Battle for Troy)*

# ISBN 978-1-7770736-6-4

No part of this guidebook shall be reproduced in any form without permission in writing from the publisher except in the case of brief quotations embodied in critical articles or reviews.

Legal & Disclaimer

The information contained in this book is not designed to replace or take the place of any form of medicine or professional medical advice. The information in this book has been provided for educational & entertainment purposes only.

The information contained in this book has been compiled from sources deemed reliable, and it is accurate to the best of the Author's knowledge; however, the Author cannot guarantee its accuracy and validity and cannot be held liable for any errors or omissions. Changes are periodically made to this book. You must consult your doctor or get professional medical advice before using any of the suggested remedies, techniques, or information in this book.

Upon using the information contained in this book, you agree to hold harmless the Author from and against any damages, costs, and expenses, including any legal fees potentially resulting from the application of any of the information provided by this guide. This disclaimer applies to any damages or injury caused by the use and application, whether directly or indirectly, of any advice or information presented, whether for breach of contract, tort, negligence, personal injury, criminal intent, or under any other cause of action.

You agree to accept all risks of using the information presented inside this book. You need to consult a professional medical practitioner in order to ensure you are both able and healthy enough to participate in this program.

## Table Of Contents

Chapter 1: The Bronze Age ...................... 1

Chapter 2: Who Were The Trojans? ......... 7

Chapter 3: The Mycenaean Greeks ........ 14

Chapter 4: The Prize Is Troy ................... 21

Chapter 5: Homer's Reason For The Trojan War ......................................................... 27

Chapter 6: 10-Year War Or Many Battles? ............................................................. 36

Chapter 7: Greeks Ready For The Fight .. 45

Chapter 8: Troy Was Safe--At Least In Appearances ......................................... 53

Chapter 9: Is The Trojan Horse Real? ..... 58

Chapter 10: The Stealthy Greeks............ 63

Chapter 11: The Battle For The City Was The Battle ............................................. 70

Chapter 12: A Horse Of A Different Color 75

Chapter 13: The Impact The Trojan Horse Created .................................................. 80

Chapter 14: The Trojans Lived, Weakened Perhaps .................... 85

Chapter 15: Origins ................. 89

Chapter 16: Gods, Goddesses And Spirits ............................. 92

Chapter 17: Short Tales Of Gods And Heroes .................... 108

Chapter 18: Flying Too High ................. 115

Chapter 19: The Complex Tale Of Oedipus And The Self-Fulfilling Prophecies ........ 118

Chapter 20: The Trojan War ................. 129

Chapter 21: The Odyssey ..................... 139

Chapter 22: The Apple Of Discord ........ 152

Chapter 23: Heroes Of The Trojan War 162

Chapter 24: The Wooden Horse ........... 170

Chapter 25: The God Of War ................ 181

**Chapter 1: The Bronze Age**

The background is essential to understand how the Trojan War was fought and the way in which the Trojan horse could be used to be victorious in the battle. When you're more familiar of this period of Bronze Age, you can start to comprehend the mystery that archeologists are now beginning to solve.

The Bronze Age is defined by the melting of the metals tin and copper or the trade of bronze-based products. The Bronze Age is also classified as being the 3rd millennium B.C. But, it means various matters based on the areas of the globe being considered.

The Near East, which categorizes these countries as follows: Anatolia, Elam, Caucasus, Egypt, Mesopotamia and the Levant and Sistan and Sistan, was a part of the Bronze Age from 3300 to 1200 B.C.

Then, it is important to be aware the fact that Anatolia was also regarded as Asia Minor. Anatolia has now become Turkey.

South Asia was said to have been in an Bronze Age from 3ooo to 1200 B.C. Europe including Aegean was in its Bronze Age in 3200 to 600 B.C. Greece was regarded as part of Europe at the time and held a monopoly over Aegean properties, and also control over the Aegean Sea.

In order to put the Bronze Age dates into perspective, Greece was a mighty power from around 1600 B.C. until the time of 1100 B.C.

Notice: A lot of historians are looking to prove their existence, including Troy as well as The Trojan War, and the Trojan Horse, believe the Bronze Age ended in 1100 B.C. in Greece as well as the Near East. It will not be debated in this book.

Based on the information provided by Troia Archeological Site site and UNESCO World Heritage Site, the site is thought as a portion of the City of Troy was inhabited between 3000 B.C. up to about 500 A.D.

The largest portion of this span of time the most important for us is between 1300 and 1000 B.C. There is a consensus that Homer's Troy as well as Troy that fell due to Troy that was destroyed due to Greece's Trojan Horse existed sometime between 1300-1150 B.C.

Carl Blegen was an archeologist who was a researcher at the location now known as Troy between 1932 until the year 1938. Blegen's chronology for the Troy Strata provides a look from 1300 to 1000 B.C.

Strata is a term used in geology which means the layers of earth that archeologists have uncovered trying to uncover archaeological evidence to aid in understanding the ancient civilisations of Troy.

The strata are classified at the site level: Troy VIh, Troy VIIa, Troy VIIb1, Troy VIIb2 as well as Troy VIIb3. There's an approximate ending date for each of the site levels which means that the culture which existed before the dates was somehow affected.

Troy VIh was said to be over around 1300 B.C. as a result of an earthquake. The buildings, the people as well as artifacts that are discovered during the time span show evidence of an important natural event like the earthquake which caused people to evacuate and abandon their everyday possessions to be left behind.

The following date to end the life of Troy the city was 1230-1190/1180 BC that is Troy VIIa. Most likely, the cause mentioned was an attack from the enemy.

At the time of the year 1150 BC, Troy VIIb1 was devastated by an unknown reason. Troy VIIb2 demolished at the end of 1100 BC or because of an earthquake or an attack from the enemy. Troy VIIb3 was destroyed around 1000 BC because of an unknown reason.

Troy VIIa is among the most significant strata. Many archeologists, such as Blegen, Schliemann, Calvert and Strauss believe that it was Troy VIIa is the Troy was mentioned in both the Iliad as well as the Odyssey thus that the Troy that was associated with the conflict was Troy VIIa. Blegen is the only one to back the assertion. While digging up the Troy VIIa, he uncovered several skeletons not yet buried. They also had Mycenaean Greek arrowheads near the corpses, suggesting that the battle took place.

The discussion continues to grow concerning Troy and Troy, the Mycenaean

Greeks, and the Trojan Horse, remember the likely "Trojan War" took place between 1230-1180 B.C. This is due to the skeletons that were not buried, carbon dating of the bones, as well as the geological evidence which provides a more narrow chronology. The primary evidence that suggests that this was the time when the war of 10 years took place, and the absence of any other explanation that led to the destruction of the city in addition to Homer's story. The timeline also provides that will be used to discuss the reason why the war began and the way it came to an end.

**Chapter 2: Who Were The Trojans?**

Most historians and archeologists believe the idea that Trojans have a mix from Anatolian and Luwian roots. But this wasn't often the case. In the past, the sole proof for the idea that Troy and Trojans had was Homer's stories. The book will keep bringing in Homer as well as the issue of history and legend, but actually in order to comprehend the complete information this book will provide, you must be familiar with the "players." provide the reader, it's necessary to know an understanding of Troy and the "players."

The account Homer wrote of the war epic in the epic war, he utilized Greek spelling of names. It is evident now that the reason he used Greek spellings was because the author was Greek and also because at the time that the epic was first written Greek was the most well-known of languages. For archeologists from earlier times who wanted to establish there was a City in Troy existed, it was a war that lasted for 10 years, which the Greeks triumphed. Any information from the epic poem of Homer in connection with historical facts was crucial.

Archeological digs have finally solved the mystery of what they Trojans truly were, free of any mythological or untrue beliefs about the history of the time. Archeologists believe that they were Trojan inhabitants were Anatolian as well as Luwian heritage due to the archaeological evidence, structures, as well as rituals.

Historical Context Uncovered by Schliemann and Others

Frank Calvert went to what today is Turkey to discover the actual City in Troy. Calvert was not a famous archeologist at the time due to the absence of money and the fact that he was a autodidactic. Heinrich Schliemann was largely considered as a fraud, and was criticized due to his beliefs that he had found Troy however, He did have money to make his dig famous to the world at large and also to inform the press that he finally discovered the true Troy. The dig took place in 1871.

The Schliemann view of Troy as nothing beyond a heap dirt, a few fragments of pottery and an unshakeable belief that the theory was correct. As with many archeologists as well as the academic scientific in the world, debating or disproving the validity of a hypothesis is a powerful thing.

The archeologists, like Blegen who made their way to Turkey at the time of 1932 were enthralled with the intention of showing that Troy existed. They discovered one-half acre of the city. The citadel was located there. Now, it's 130 years after Schliemann discovered his mound and we are in 1988. Strauss and other did their bit to discover the entire area of 75 acres of urban.

In the 1930s historians believed in the 1930s that Troy was just a city on the shores of Turkey but not the lavish fortress that Greeks were afraid of. But, fifty years later, after more excavations, more strata being discovered and finally reaching the Troy VIIa area, it became discovered it was just much as huge as Homer described in his epic story. At this time that the origins of where Troy came from and where Troy was derived from were discovered.

The City Layout, Pottery, and Burials

In the event that all of the city of Troy discovered by archeologists excavations could start to reveal the Trojans' roots. The city's layout was Anatolian construction. The location of the citadel in relation to other buildings, and its architecture symbolized the Anatolian style more than Mycenaean Greek culture.

A lot of pottery has been discovered. In addition, most of these pieces were associated with the Anatolian connection. However, most pieces belonged more with Greece. Due to the transport routes used by products that came from Asia via the Aegean Sea and beyond the strait of Troy was founded It is likely that merchants from Greece traded their ceramics in Troy.

The excavations of archeological digs revealed burial sites in the area, which suggested Anatolian burial methods versus practices of the Greeks.

If you take into account the place of the city situated located in Anatolia which is also known as Turkey then it makes sense to consider the Trojans to descend from the earlier Anatolian people.

Evidence suggests an even larger Greek populace lived in Troy However, this was just after when the Trojan War is thought to be taking place. The evidence comes from strata of artifacts the case of Greek artifacts were discovered within strata that were closer to the high point that Trojan artifacts.

Where Science Has Yet to Reach

DNA mapping is now feasible. Many species, including humans are being tracked to discover their the origins. There is a lot to know about bones found in prehistoric times are now known through DNA. But the skeletons that were discovered in Troy and believed to be involved during this Trojan War have yet to be tested for DNA, or at least, they have been made available to the general public for use.

In analyzing DNA information to determine confirmation, it appears that scientists have gotten all the way back to finding the source from the Etruscans. It is only mentioned in order to demonstrate that the Trojan lineage did not go out entirely. DNA evidence indicates Etruscan heritage is linked to Hittite as well as the Lydian Kingdoms. Troy was one of both kingdoms. Further details about the Hittites will be explained in chapter on the reasons why the Trojan War occurred.

Due to the enormous interest shown in Troy within the world of academia there is a good chance that DNA testing of the skeletons discovered in Troy City of Troy will someday be done in order to address more questions regarding the time as well as the people living in the area.

The simplest answer for what were the Trojans is: Anatolian descendants.

**Chapter 3: The Mycenaean Greeks**

There is always two major players and, in some cases, others, because they have agreements with the principal parties fighting. This could be redundant to talk about what the Greeks were. If we talk about the Trojans There is a problem because of the assumption that early on they were ancestors of Greece but in actual fact they were not. Trojans were more than their Anatolian origin.

It is possible to say, "duh they were Greeks." Did you know that there existed Mycenaean Greeks and Dorian Greeks who lived during the Bronze Age? Are you aware that cities such as Pylos as well as Athens were home to Mycenaean Greeks and many of the Dorian Greeks had started to move out of Greece which weakened their position as they moved towards Europe?

In all societies, there are obvious differences, sometimes even within a general term that refers to a specific source. One great illustration shows the current trend is to label someone who comes is a mistake to label someone from Korea is akin to calling someone from Korea Asian. True, Asia as the continent of Asia is vast and encompasses a variety of people, with different backgrounds in their faith, manner of living, and even their language. Chinese is distinct from Korean and so is Japanese as well as Japanese, which is distinct from the other two languages. It is therefore crucial to understand who is who the Mycenaean Greeks were.

The Mycenaean Period

The Mycenaean period was an time that the Greek mainland was in the midst of the power and riches of Greece. The most powerful cities included Mycenae, Thebes,

Tiryns Thebes, Tiryns and Athens. Greek workshops were full of pottery and bronze as well as jewelry and carved gems vase, glass decorations as well as precious metals.

It is believed that the Mycenaean Greeks had a wide market for their trade, shipping products from Greece throughout the Mediterranean and extending it beyond Spain all the way to Levant. The evidence from that time shows that vessels as well as wine, oil and vases were the main commodities of trade.

The Greeks were not just traders. They were warriors as well as engineers. They built monuments in the shape of beehives, bridges as well as fortification walls made of Cyclopean stone. The Mycenaean's also developed irrigation and drainage networks. Mycenae was considered to be the city that was rich in gold while Pylos was a sandy city (Homer's account).

Evidence from tablets that were used for preserving historical events by scribes, suggested Greece was very well-organized feudal system. As per Colette Hemingway as well as Sean Hemingway, the late 1300th century B.C. or the 1200s was the time in decline for The Mycenaean Greeks. Important sites, that were awash with riches were destroyed, and Mycenaeans began moving into remote areas. Pylos that was the main city of the king was destroyed around 1200 B.C. It isn't totally gone since it remains located situated in Greece known as Pylos-Nestoras currently.

Historical scholars believe that the total decline that occurred during the time of Mycenaean Greeks occurred by the beginning the year 1100 B.C., while many city collapses during the period 1300-1180 B.C. threatened ultimate destruction. The war was also the time that saw the rebuilding of areas of cities that in which the Greeks believed were crucial.

There's a little controversy over the debate at this time and some historians believe it was the populace movements that rendered the Mycenaeans weakness. People studying more deeply the Trojan War are more inclined to conclude that it was internal conflicts and also a desire to stretch their resources in order to conquer cities that were important for shipping.

Other Important Players

The world was not made up solely of Trojans or Mycenaean Greeks. There was plenty of conflict, natural disasters and wars within the country that began to alter the existing kingdoms, a step beyond the events that occurred within Troy or Mycenaean Greek cities.

The Hittites ruled the kingdom of power, and comprised Troy. At the exact time

Troy was destroyed, Hattusa, the capital of the Hittite Kingdom was destroyed. Aramaic nomads as well as Chaldeans threatened the existence of both the Assyrian as well as Babylonian empires. There was a Dorian Greek invasion. Dorian Greeks were migrating and expanding, creating trouble to The Mycenaean Greeks.

The idea was that Mycenaean's as well as the Hittites enjoyed an uneasy relationship due to mutual respect and anxiety about destruction. A peace agreement among Hittite Kings Hattusili III, and the King of Ahhiyawa from the Mycenaean Greeks existed.

But, Egyptian factions and others such as Piyama-Radu fought constantly against those of the Hittite Kingdom. The two civilizations wanted to spread out of Africa to Asia however this was complicated because it was a challenge because the

Hittite wall fortresses were robust. King Ahhiyawa received Lesbos by the Piyama-Radu in the 13th century B.C. Piyama-Radu was even attempting to get into Troy in order to reach the capital city of the Hittite Kingdom.

There is evidence that suggests that the relationship between Piyama-Radu was much more significant for the Greeks as was keeping tranquility in the presence of Hittite King. Even though there was an extended time following the time that King Hattusili III pleaded for peace, Ahhiyawa was able to agree to accept.

## Chapter 4: The Prize Is Troy

A look at the map of globe today and all its nations, Turkey is north of the Mediterranean Sea. It was Anatolia in the time of the Trojan War it was a territory ruled by the force from the Hittite Kingdom. In between Greece as well as Turkey are the Aegean Sea. The region is divided by the Dardanelles A narrow strait leading towards the Sea of Marmara and then through a second strait to the Black Sea. The opening of the Black Sea meant trade ships could travel to east Europe, Russia, and the present-day state of Georgia.

Greece had power over Greece was the dominant power in Mediterranean as well as the Aegean Seas. Since it was a huge trader and a world-class engineering powerhouse such as their vessels that were built, it was easy to Greece to regulate both seas.

The only thing that stopped Greece from exploring the east of Asia The land located on the opposite side of the Dardanelles and the city of Troy was able to protect.

The land was regarded as to be blessed because water was plentiful. Water that was clean and drinkable was vital and Troy could draw the water. The soil was ideal to grow grains and support livestock. Seas were full of fish that ensured Trojans could eat plenty.

The Trojans were thought of as middlemen in the shipping business. The city was unable trading other than the sale of the manufacture of textiles and horses. Indeed, Troy was known for its exceptionally well-bred horses. Troy was gaining wealth due to the control of travel across the river and because of the winds of Boreas.

In the 30-60 days in the summer months, the winds could blow, making trading easier within trade in Aegean Sea, across the strait and up to through the Sea of Marmara and into the Black Sea. If the winds stopped the ships were not able to sail since they were not capable of tacking or going in a zigzag fashion.

Captains of ship would be required to make a docking at Troy in the event that winds ceased. It could be for one period of time or for a few days vessels would be docked at Troy. Of course, this meant trade. Trojans were able to provide meals and accommodation for the captains of these vessels and crew.

Conflict over middlemen earning rich was evident. Greece obviously desired the fortress to expand their wealth and also to gain entry into to the Hittite community. Troy was an ideal location to provide defense from the west of those in the Hittite kingdom.

There is a clear indication in numerous texts both fiction and written histories that Greek saw Troy as a danger and attraction. Trojans represented a danger due to the possibility of them deciding to move across the strait to Greece and attempt to take over cities. Troy might also attempt to control the Aegean Sea, and then become stronger in the maritime community.

When you look at historical records that Troy was an important victory for numerous rival forces. In sifting through the layers of dirt to discover the story of Troy it's evident Troy was a prize to be won. Trojans were involved in numerous battles at the start in the Bronze Age till the end of Troy being a city by the year 500 AD.

It's All About Location and Desire

The most popular theory of how it was that Trojan War occurred, either as a war lasting 10 years or a few small, intense combats lasting 10 years it is because Troy was a sought-after place for those who were Mycenaean Greeks.

The Greeks were keen on expanding and gaining control over a rich city. Why would a middleman be wealthy in the event that it was more beneficial to own the citadel as well as the city? With the city's ownership it was easier to access the Hittite Kingdom, Asia Minor and all of Asia was made easier.

The greatest leaders and warriors could be thinking of this regardless of whether they considered daily life their top essential part of their lives. The coincidence of the position of Troy as well as the need to build a country that would benefit through controlling trade in shipping could have resulted in the Mycenaean Greeks developing strategy after plan to eventually slay Troy and bring down the reign of Trojans.

One of the main reasons that it was that the Trojan War began, was constantly fought, and eventually ended, was the need to control the place and to make Troy the ultimate prize.

## Chapter 5: Homer's Reason For The Trojan War

The epic battle it was recorded in the Iliad and continued in the Odyssey and recounted in various works of writers over time According to Homer the battle was started because of the woman.

Helen of Troy A beauty far unlike any other, has been said to have initiated the conflict between Mycenaean Greeks and Troy. Helen as per Homer is one of the daughters of Zeus. Helen was the Greek goddess, the wife of Agamemnon and also the Prince of Troy's Paris lovers.

The Iliad describes an official trip Paris made to the kingdom of Agamemnon in Greece. The story goes that Paris was on the trip to establish a more favorable relations with Greece and Troy to facilitate trade. Many believe that the purpose of his visit was to reassure Agamemnon that

Troy would not be a threat to Greece. Trojans will not rebel against Greece.

The issue with this tale is the fact that it's an epic poem that was composed by Homer basing his work on various aspects of history. However, it was and not all of them in the period 1300-1180 B.C. Homer was born centuries before the supposed 10 years of Trojan War.

We now know that we know that the Trojan War was at least an event. However, the question about whether it was a 10-year-long war similar to the epic battle in Homer's tales or tiny, fierce skirmishes that lasted for over 10 years, is in the process of being resolved.

The scholars of archeology, history and literature will be sure that a war, or sequence of wars took over Troy. Troy in the period between 1230-1180. The evidence, which is coming into the light during the 90s and 2000s. It suggesting that the battles that put an end to in the end Trojans as a group and their culture occurred between 1180 and 1200 B.C.

We know the approximate date it happened, the length of battle and the location. Also, we know some details about the principal players since the included Mycenaean Greeks and Trojans.

The process of determining the primary reason based on the literature, as well as the few historic records that are available It is more difficult. Was Helen of Troy really exist as a real person, and was she not a mythological God, Homer made her appear to be? There aren't any records of her in Mycenaean Greek or Trojan history which speak of a woman known as Helen.

Do you think this means she can't be true? Absolutely not, women of the earlier times, and even from the early 1900s onwards were viewed as inferior sexual partner. Women were worshipped as goddesses, however, females in the human race were thought to be much superior to males. If we believe that the spouse of the present Greek King actually existed and that she escaped with the prince of Troy and returned to Troy, then we can suppose that the Greeks felt humiliated by this blatant incident. There is also the possibility that Troy had ended its existence as a result of this act, could not record its historical record and was equally shamed of their Prince. There is plenty of presuming to do.

A line of evidence to the Homer story of Helen of Troy can be discovered in Hittite archives, which identify Akagamunas, the king of Ahhiyawa at the time of the period of 14th century B.C. Based on the spelling and translation to Greek it could be referring to the Homer story of Agamemnon.

## Historic Records from a Variety of Cultures

There are a variety of civilizations that date back to the dawn of humankind which suggest that there was a war fought for women. The kings considered their daughters to be wedding sacrifices to rival kingdoms. In more recent times, the notion of marrying the princess or queen to a king or prince was used to ensure peace between the two nations. The history of England reflects this quite effectively.

If the princess or the royal woman did not agree, this would constitute a cause for the outbreak of war. There is also the possibility that the princess was offered as a gift to the peace of God and a plan was put in place for gaining access to the royal family and be able to take over the kingdom by waging a war that was less difficult.

Another more pertinent notion is that of that of the Middle Eastern wars, occurring mostly because of religious differences. True there is a reason that the "war against terror" is being waged in the wake of 9-11. However, there's a second reason that is related with "women's rights" and aiding women suffering, or are not believed to enjoy the same rights. This isn't to argue about this ongoing, important battle, but rather to emphasize the fact that "women's rights" are often cited as an excuse for soldiers to stay within this region of the Middle East. This gives credence to conflicts being waged with an excuse that cites a woman or woman as a catalyst or the primary reason behind fighting.

There is a good chance that war might be fought on behalf of a woman who fled between her husband and the prince of a different country. At present, it's an idea based mostly on Homer's narrative regarding his experience during the Trojan War.

If we accept his story as historically correct and complete except for gods and goddesses as well as other elements of mythology, it is necessary to accept it was the case that Trojan War was waged due to the actions of a woman and the actions of a Trojan prince.

An Excuse to Sack Troy

It's possible that it is possible that the Mycenaean Greeks used a woman as a reason to battle the Trojans at their home. The Mycenaean king might have had his most powerful warriors to board their most powerful ships, and then attack the citadel in an try to gain access to the city. This would be an excellent excuse to fulfill the well-known desire Greeks wanted to achieve Troy and the control of the Dardanelles.

Its Homer-esque story is a beautiful and tragic story of a city coming to its knees due to a woman, creates a fascinating historical account as opposed to the standard version that might have been recorded.

What will the solution to the questionof what caused the Trojans battle against Mycenaean Greeks occur and end with defeat for Troy? Troy will ever be revealed? This is highly likely. Even after 145 years, an answers are still elusive. There's a myriad of theories and doubts being proposed by archeologists and historians due to the evidence is not sufficient.

If we suppose Homer composed a poem about a woman in real life and gave her the name Helen to shield the various parties that were later involved, we could conclude that the catalyst for war was the woman.

If we believe that the woman was not there, then Greeks discovered a second catalyst that allowed them for advancing through the walls Troy until at last they were Greeks won against the formidable citadel as well as the Troy warriors. Troy.

The final reasons for the war is yours as the reader to determine based on both the place as a cause for fighting and the fact that it was known in history that women were a good excuse for the kings of England to start war against different kingdoms.

**Chapter 6: 10-Year War Or Many Battles?**
It is believed that the Trojan War is considered a 10 year siege of Troy. City of Troy that ended when it was over when the Trojan Horse was rolled into the city, surrounded by Greeks. It could not be the epic 10-year struggle described in Homer's epic poetry. How does this impact how the war ended if it was not a constant ten-year battle? It could certainly impact the legitimacy and authenticity of the Trojan horse as well as what was supposed to be accomplished by the Greek invention.

If the truth of the Homer myth is proven to be utterly false the logic is that to conclude that the Trojan horse might be just an imaginative fable also. The challenge the archeologists and historians had being convinced that they were able to believe that the Trojan War was actually a true battle is due to the manner of life in the time the story was believed to have occurred.

It is not a secret that wars were fought regularly. No matter if you study Egypt, Greece, Troy and the Hittite Kingdom, Ancient China or any other historical period of a community or population group. It was just as normal every day like eating.

Human nature's basic need to live, thrive and achieve happiness was the driving force behind nations across the globe throughout the Bronze Age. In order for a nation to prevail against another one, strength strategies, strategy, as well as fighting was required. Only the most powerful or most experienced who could endure the battles that an adversary could begin. The fear of losing was definitely a driving power.

The fear that another person was going to take the initiative first. The fear of your opponent having more power or intelligence or having a better plan was common. Children, adults, women were unable to go about their lives every day and feel safe. Not the way we think now.

In a time when war is a distance away, it's simple to overlook that there are people dying for the sake of their religion or because they did the wrong move or said an untruthful thing towards the wrong individual. When we lived in the Bronze Age, it was difficult to overlook the possibility of death when you sleep while awake or even when attempting to escape fighting.

Combat is still ongoing in the world, regardless of an interruption somewhere in between. Take a second to think about World War II and Christmas Eve. One evening, both troops were singing and ceased fighting. Next day, peace had ended and the fighting resumed.

North Korea and South Korea have been fighting for supremacy in there is a Demilitarized Zone lay between the frontiers. One nation is permanently divided in two until a calamity occurs to disrupt the fragile peace.

In the past, when we discussed about the Mycenaean Greeks, their relationships and strength, in addition to those of Troy You know that battles continued to be fought. If it wasn't Egypt seeking to conquer into the Hittite Kingdom and destroy its capital city, it could be the Greeks in fear of Trojan expansion. Or in the opposite direction. There was definitely fighting between Greeks and Trojans that might have begun because of women or men.

One must find out is if that conflict was continuous for ten lengthy years, or was an intense series of combats which ended in the annihilation of Troy VIIa.

A Series of Battles is More Likely

According to the article, life was tough for the people who lived during the Bronze Age. The concept of unlimited supplies was not one that was in use. The journey by ship can take up to a half year since the wind could be slowed for a few days during the voyage.

People's longevity was considerably lower due to the effects of famine, illness, war or natural catastrophes. The growth in population, though important at the time however, didn't necessarily mean that there was always enough soldiers to wage an ongoing fight.

One battle that was fought in the presence of Trojans shooting arrows into the heart of Greeks below, could have wiped the entire fleet out and ended the conflict. A new army would need to be brought in to replace the deceased, but could Greece be able to spare the warriors needed to fight for 10 years?

Greece was not the only country with borders as well as other relations and internal conflicts to deal with. The truth is that Greece could not sustain the practice of sending troops, year after year over ten years, trying to conquer Troy.

Most likely efforts were launched during a time when Greece was in fear and they had a reason to fight or to maintain peace on the country they resided in permitted them to try once more to bring down their Trojan society.

This one army comprised of hundreds of thousands of soldiers was able to continue attacking every day and on until the Trojan horse came to be and is 99 percent not possible according to archeologists who study Troy.

Supporting Facts

In the previous chapter on the strata layers you were taught that Troy was repeatedly destroyed. At times, the city was destroyed by natural disasters which caused an explosion and Trojans abandoned the city then returning to construct it once more.

In the period between 1300 and ten00 B.C., archeological evidence cannot establish that a lengthy, never endless war that was fought against Troy. It is clear that it was the effects of a natural catastrophe, the attack of an enemy as well as unidentified reasons for destruction, additional problems with natural disasters or enemies as well as other unidentified reasons that caused the city's destruction to cease.

It is also proven that between 1180 and 1200, Mycenaean Greeks finally entered Troy. They occupied the city Troy in the year 1180, and massacred a lot of Trojans and then left them in ruins as they left an impressive and mighty city.

The earth layer over the earth at this time indicates that the city was rebuilt and to be destroyed over and over again in the form of new cities, until around 500 AD Troy was abandoned forever.

Based on the information we have about life in society between 1230-1150 B.C. Historical scholars can suggest with some certainty that the siege was actually a sequence of battles that culminated in the final battle being a brilliant one. The issue of whether Troy was ever a real place, or whether there was any sort of conflict, can be addressed.

Are you sure? Homer did or is it what people remain to argue about as the truth? No it's not completely. The proof of one theory above an acceptable doubt isn't feasible given the limited documents that are available about Troy and the time it ended in the 1180s B.C.

It would be great to have an archeological idea proposed by those who were digging at Troy can be confirmed as valid. It would bring to an end the discussion regarding what could or might be. What we will need to do is understand that there were wars as well as natural catastrophes. Troy was built repeatedly until the city was eventually abandoned, forgotten and covered in soil layers that would have been torn by Boreas winds, as desired by captains of ships in that Bronze Age.

**Chapter 7: Greeks Ready For The Fight**

The first point of reference for all data pertaining to Trojan War is always Homer's incredible epic poem. This may be irritating to keep talking about this but, you must understand that in order how to talk about a historical narrative that relates to this Trojan War, one has always refer to the text Homer composed and all subsequent writers. The Aeneid is a different story that uses the ideas of that of the Trojan War based on Homer's work. Instead of getting lost by the many books which have been published, it's time to think about what could be the events that occurred during those ten lengthy years of battle.

If it were really 10 years long in the past, the Greek army was required to be prepared for battle that they planned to fight from the sea. The Dardanelles Strait measures 38 miles long, and ranges between 0.75 to four miles across. A mile today and even up to 4 miles doesn't seem like an ideal trip. This can be accomplished in just a couple of minutes on the motorized boats available today. Ferries who travel across this region daily, go through it often throughout the each day.

However, in the past however, this wasn't in the past. Greek ships, although technologically advanced, remained under the influence of sails and a lot of men were rowing oars within the hold. The historical records suggest that the Bireme was a kind that was a Greek warship, was in use during the Trojan War.

It was a huge vessel, having thirty oars, or more to each side. many men necessary to drive this boat across the ocean. The front of the ship was designed with a triangular design, and the back was turned upwards to secure the sail into the right position. It was a larger and narrower vessel than sailboats that we are acquainted with today. It also had only one mast. It had the sail running parallel to its length vessel and not perpendicular.

The ships were designed for skimming over waters and were not designed to move lots of water. The ships' hulls were shorter than sailing boats which came years later. The building needed to be wider, so that ships could move easily through the waters, but even that could take quite a long time.

The historical accounts don't mention the possibility of a route to get from Greece to Troy beyond a ships. Although the Greeks knew how to build bridges, it is no proof that they would have built an extension bridge that was about a mile long that would connect Greece into what is today Turkey.

Biremes weren't designed to haul supplies. They were designed for transporting warriors who needed power to move the ships over the ocean. This was a exhausting task. Imagine spending days rowing in the hope that the wind will aid, and then finally arriving at Troy.

The armada could be visible, or even the Trojans may have been anticipating the ship to come. The people who watched from the citadel could have seen the Greek warships as they were since trade vessels were quite different in size and shape.

Furthermore, if conflict was started by Paris or the prince of Troy truly was, Troy was likely that it was time to get ready to fight the Greek troops. This also happened at an time that demand was put forth. It was a matter of honor to demand the return of an Greek citizen prior to the start of an war.

The men had to consider strategies and whether or not they could win the war whatever the cause that it started. According to this research there is a high probability of being 100percent certain that the Trojans had a clue that they were fighting Greeks were headed to fight another war when they reached the shores.

The ideal place for ships to land was within the harbor that was protected and it was a constant source of shipping activity when the winds were not conducive to travel. A ship's mooring elsewhere might have been difficult even if it was not nearly impossible. This may be costly for the Greek their vessels.

It wasn't as if the construction of an Greek warship could be completed in a day or within just a couple of weeks. It required time to gather the wood, then mill the wood, then form it into the vessel.

There are some accounts that suggest Trojans could meet the Greeks in the course of battle, fight before returning to their fortress. the Greeks returned to their boats. This is an option. There were spaces outside the city walls which could have served as battlefields. combat.

If you look at Homer's writing works, as well as films such as Troy trying to show the epic battle that is based upon the known facts from the time, it's possible that an opulent war series was fought.

Trojan men could have made their way through the city's gates, held their ground and prevented the Greeks from entering the city. Trojans might also have been on the walls of the fortress as they hurled fireballs as well as arrows and hot oil on the Greeks who tried to get into the citadel and into the city.

It is also difficult to give any exact information, or in any detail on how conflict was waged. The only thing we can say is what's written in the texts. Homer believed that Trojans came together in battle fighting, died, and held the Greeks from advancing every time.

The Greeks as they prepared for battle, might bring some provisions, however, not enough for up to ten years. Ships carrying supplies could be granted access in periods of conflict or on rest times. The men could not be fighting all day long, every night.

If it was possible to have enough troops to create reserve warriors, it might be difficult to fight fighting in dark night. It is a mistake for either or both the Greeks and Trojans to have battled during the night.

The armour wasn't comfortable and easy to maneuver inside. Being able to see by moonlight and fire was not a guarantee that victory would be achieved. The general consensus was that war must be conducted in a manner that was based on honor and the right strategy.

The unexpected attack of inducing the enemy into an underworld was acceptable however, each one of them required time to recover the wounded and dead and show respect to the fallen who fell.

The question of whether the Greeks were able to return home each time there was a war played out and ultimately lost, isn't clear. According to Homer the Greeks stayed close to Troy and also on Trojan fields. Homer claims that fighting took place in fields which were usually filled with water. This could be made fighting more difficult or even impossible for the two sides.

## Chapter 8: Troy Was Safe--At Least In Appearances

In the midst of 10 or more years of war that never stopped there was a feeling that the Greeks were gone in the sense of poetry. Homer recounts the Greek ships that left the harbor following a final fight, presumably knowing that they had been defeated and knowing that Troy was not able to be defended.

Homer was also a writer of the gift left behind by his father. An icon, relic or a gift for the Trojans believed to represent peace. In the end, it appeared that to be the case that the Greeks might leave and allow Helen to remain in Paris but peace would be restored for the duration of time.

However, it could not have been the case anyhow. Many historians are inclined to believe that Homer's story is correct is due to that of the Trojan horse. Before you get too confident about the subject of the Trojan horse and the debate to have for a final conclusion on the battle, it's important to think about how the Trojans could be able to bring gifts inside the citadel's gates in the event that the Greeks weren't around.

If you are given a gift one is prone to think that you will accept the gift. The last thing you want is to be rude or disrespectful towards the person who is giving the present. If an extended war of ten years took place it is possible to conclude that your opponent has finally exhausted their tactics or that they were no longer able to go on in the fight.

But, it is likely that you'd be reluctant to take a gift particularly if a large portion of the Greek army was not yet inside your gates. This would suggest to assume that the Greeks would be eager to be waiting in love with the present, and then to unlock the door to strike.

It is believed that the Trojan horse is thought to be an ideal strategy to take over the city of a few soldiers due to the fact that it was left in the form of a present, and Greeks were able to retreat. It's an easy task for a leader exhausted from war and apprehensive that war had been sorted out.

This is certainly the most effective technique in the history of mankind that was used when the Greeks abandoned as well as the Trojans were a victim of this strategy. In a false belief that there was an ending to any war regardless of whether it was the end of the long series of intermittent fighting or the more than ten years of combat that was the most likely defeat of Troy.

Debating if the Greek Army Actually Left

There are some historians who think that the Greek army was not able to depart. Instead, they suggest using an ax, instead of an actual Trojan horse, these historians consider that the Greeks were able to pass through the city's gates.

It's a plausible scenario that is just as probable it is it is to imagine a Trojan horse that was built and then abandoned on the doorstep of Troy. In the absence of regular breaks to recuperate from different battles and battles, the Greeks might have returned back to their homes several times in order to prepare the next battle.

Animals who are caged, and find it difficult to stay in the cage are likely to test each inch of their cages to find weak spots. If there is a weakness discovered after the tests, animals will utilize it as a way to get out. The Greeks might have studied and tested for over 10 years in order to discover the most vulnerable point of Troy's fortress. They broke through and then sacked the city.

It's hard to tell because the city's walls are gone. What remains of Troy VIIa that was said to be present at the time of the Trojan War, are ruins. Much like the other documents from the time in time There isn't much data to prove this epic work Homer composed. What a story of glory, Homer composed.

The city felt safe A present brimming with Greeks as well as the demise of a culture.

## Chapter 9: Is The Trojan Horse Real?

A special program covering the Trojan War and the horse that brought the war to an end has given new proof to scholars. archeologists are still digging in Troy's city Troy have discovered what they call the actual Trojan horse.

The archeologists claim to discovered several petrified wood pieces, which form what is known as the Trojan horse. The wood's curve and the holes that hold the nails and the amount of wood pieces found will be the basis of what we imagine as the Trojan horse.

It's difficult to argue the authenticity of picture-documentation as well as the content of a PBS special and archeologists who worked tirelessly to find clues about this Trojan War and the famed horse.

The scholars can, consequently, admit that Troy wasn't quite as safe in the sense that

Trojans would have believed. The Greeks actually did offer a gift stuffed of Greek soldiers.

What was the method by which Greek soldiers create the gift they gave to their soldiers, so fast and with out the Trojans having a prickly view about such an undertaking? Looking back to Homer we learn that they made it all just one evening using the materials of several from the Greek ships.

It's hard to believe that the horse could be constructed in a single night. The idea of building the Trojan horse using boat material seems to be plausible. That would have been the only thing they could have. If a vessel was lost in one of the battles it's not difficult to imagine it was later rebuilt as a "gift."

There were many Greeks lost in conflicts Also, it's likely to be the case that Greek warriors would have utilized the vessels without concern for the people on board. The fewer people who returned alive means that fewer ships were brought back as these warriors also were responsible for the ship's capability to maneuver.

Prior to the discovery of the planks in the citadel, a variety of theories about was the Trojan horse was actually, were proposed. Many believed that they were constructed with modular pieces large enough to accommodate men and then with a slight change in form, they added the horse's head as well as legs on the side of the vessel.

Some scholars believed that they were merely the battering ram. It was also named with a specific name, since such items were commonplace at the time. The same scholars believed Homer had a wrong understanding of what "Trojan horse" signified, therefore naturally

Homer drew a huge horse and a group of men for a representation of the military coup.

An iconic structure that inspired legends and legends, the Trojan horse was extremely significant in the final days of the Trojan civilisation. There is evidence to suggest that it was real and in the form of a horse that contained people remains a source of curiosity. There's even been a evidence suggesting that the Greeks originally thought of creating mallards, and rather than the Trojan horse, it could be the Trojan duck, which rolled through Troy. Troy and brought about the most famous ending to the epic fight. The purpose of this story is to demonstrate that it doesn't matter regardless of the weapon used such as a battering-ram, an old wooden horse or even a duck, the strategy used by the Greeks is incredibly effective.

It has also shaped numerous wars that have followed, however we won't get to the idea of war yet.

**Chapter 10: The Stealthy Greeks**

In the Trojan horse, there were ten brave men, as per Homer. Maybe, there were some more, or maybe lesser. It is important to understand the method of execution. Although they could have tried for 10 years or years but the Greeks were unable to enter Troy's city Troy and stop to the Trojan King and his family. Following the earthquake and reconstruction up until about 1180, Troy was thriving; Trojans continued to fight in battles and prevail.

It was an time where the Greeks were required to develop an effective strategy, or be defeated once more. They had to be afraid that Trojans might one day make an excursion across the Dardanelles on their own battleships, and then attempt to conquer Greece.

It was the Mycenaean Greeks were suffering their own collapse and death.

Pylos was devastated. A growing number of residents left the main cities because of natural disasters or perhaps illness or perhaps a need to leave.

Historical accounts reveal that how the Mycenaean Greek civilizations, as they were known as in the early 1300s B.C., were losing the strength they once had. If they didn't see a change then they'd be at the end of their culture and not the Trojans.

There were many battles to be fought and test runs within the walls of the fortresses of Troy and Troy, it's only reasonable to think that the Greeks were experimenting with strategies after strategies, before they came up with a strategy which will never cease to amaze the any new civilisation.

We may not know the nature of what the Trojan horse did, though the evidence indicates it was exactly the way Homer stated, but we do know that Greeks had the slyness to swindle the Trojans into admitting them to the city.

The skeletons that were not buried are found within the city have been found. It is often argued to the effect that Mycenaean Greek arrowheads were not connected to the skeletons that lay in city streets. but, it's plausible from the oral histories poetry, the actual Trojan horses that the Trojan were indeed in the city.

It was an ideal way for Greeks to gain victory in the battle. The Trojans were unaware in the majority of cases definitely rolled their present into the citadel. They were also shocked to be shocked by the unexpected arrival of Greek soldiers to be massacred.

What happened next is speculation. Could the Trojans simply taken into the present, left the area unattended, with only some warriors, and then go on with their lives? Could it be that they had been partying after the Greeks weren't there? Perhaps they were eating a meal as they saw the Greeks were able to get from the horse to prepare for their shocking assault.

It makes sense that the majority of Trojan warriors weren't around receiving the present. There were a few who guarded it in order to prevent that something unheard of was happening and were then enslaved by the Greeks emerging from the horse.

It's highly likely that, after guards were killed, the Greeks were able to open their doors for their combatants. It is more logical to have the whole Greek force that was residing nearby to have returned at night, docked at the docks and headed towards the gates of the fortress as they fought off the city.

The war of the time wasn't the same as what it is today in regards to technologies or weapons. Night vision would be quite challenging. It was not possible to kill with other weapons that swords, fire and arrows was less likely. Guns, for instance, were not available at the time. More warriors are allowed into the city, more likely it is to stop the fighting in an instant.

The idea that killing the chief, everything else stops, is not the way a war should be resolved, even if it did. The battles of the time focused on knightly chivalry. The battles were one-on-one fights, bows and arches and sword fighting. After the day, the battle was put in a standstill for the wounded to receive treatment and the soldiers to get ready for battle.

Trojans might have been furious about the deception and bewildered by the shame that this deceit resulted in. This was also an time that slaves were captured. Anyone who survived Trojans could had been enslaved and made slaves for the Greeks.

We are unable to see the whole fight, and we are only able to guess at the events that occurred, it's your decision whether the whole Greek army landed in the city at night. From a military perspective it's logical that the Greeks to remain at a location in their vessels that they Trojans were unable to view. It is also logical that their vessels would be returning towards Greece for a limited time before darkness set in and for the Greeks to turn their boats over at a certain time to a set time to be able to greet their allies in the city.

The aspect that's the most significant in the deceit actually lies in the lie, not what actually transpired after the horse had been inside. If the coup was unsuccessful and the Greeks were killed inside the horse, the plan and deceit which became the basis of subsequent wars might not have occurred in the exact same manner.

The reason is that the strategy made history altered in the way we fight combat. The heroes, the chivalry, as well as the battles between gentlemen on battlefields that always concluded with supper time were not instantly changed. Certain things changed however.

## Chapter 11: The Battle For The City Was The Battle

There is no doubt that the forces tried to break into Troy and take out the middlemen. Troy was a feared civilization. Trojans were a culture to be feared just because they had an area of land that was protected by the coastal area for The Hittite Kingdom. They had plenty of foes and also were Trojan allies.

By combining historical documents and accounts, it's evident that war was an ongoing element of the daily living. There is no doubt that Troy or the city with another name was built time and time again on the location, which is known as Hissarlik in a few textual evidence.

The accounts are all known that date back to that time from 1300 B.C. between 1300 B.C. and 1000 B.C. and 1000 B.C. Troy was a fortress which was difficult to enter. The most prominent event that is mentioned is to be the Trojan War, where the adversaries attacked and the city was devastated. There were other endings for the cities constructed on the same spot resulted from natural disasters. This is to say the fact that some of the destruction was caused, but the cause is unclear to date.

The main point of all these assertions is that the Greek army required inside the city. Homer and other evidence mentions that it was very difficult to the Greeks to penetrate the walls of the fortress and gain entry in to the city. The same sources make it appear impossible for Greeks to gain access to the king of Troy and bring an end to his rule.

The debate could continue all day long and throughout time, and there is no doubt been suggested that one of the reasons that the Greeks were so keen on Troy was the alliance they had with the Hittites, as well as the place of the city for the protection of from the Hittite Kingdom.

A significant aspect is the fact that the Greeks created the Trojan horse to allow them to eventually enter the city. Over half of the battle which the challenge that Greeks were able to win was by making sure they could get through the wall of sand and be able to reach the Trojan fighters and end their fight totally.

The Trojan horse is the instrument that helped make this take place. Whatever tool employed, the fact that it functioned is what made the history of our time was transformed to the Trojans.

The war was finished when Greeks were in. It was extremely difficult to the Trojan soldiers to take the victory in the event that they weren't smart enough to be patient and wait for a unexpected attack. We are aware that the Trojans were taken on the run, killed and the city was destroyed therefore they weren't smart enough to be able to discern their attack, which allowed the fight to win as quickly after they had rolled their horse in their city.

It's true that there were still battles that had to be fought. The Trojan warriors needed to go down or at a minimum, be willing to be submissive and accept loss. Without the Trojan horse, which allowed them to enter the city, this wouldn't be the case.

Imagine someone repeatedly knocking on your door and asking for access to the house, only to be denied time repeatedly. Think about the tactics employed by notorious serial killers that killed their victims inside their home. The victims were enticed by a scheme which appeared innocent and wasn't dangerous to them in the least. The intruder is spotted and the victim dies as a result.

But, even if the victim was denied entry, reported to the police, and was safe in a place where the criminal was unable to reach them, they could not have been ended. In this way, it clarifies that were the Trojans refused to allow to welcome the Greeks to enter under the pretense of offering a present and a gift, the city could last for several additional years, perhaps a few more years, or even grow into a greater strength.

The same about the Trojans. The Trojans were unaware of the dangers lurking within the galloping horse's stomach permitted the foe to attack and that was the conclusion of the war. The only thing the Greeks required to do was locate all their warriors to fight, wound or kill and they had the city to themselves.

## Chapter 12: A Horse Of A Different Color

We're sorry for playing with wordplay in the chapter's title however it was difficult to ignore. It is possible that the Trojan War or sequence of wars could have concluded differently to the people of Troy. According to Homer Had the Trojans had followed the guidance from certain people, the coup might not have succeeded.

An approach that is regarded as a simple one in our current time but was a masterpiece because of its simplicity, up to the point where it actually performed. It was rare for any kind of strategy to play a role in the combats that were fought in the Bronze Age. The battles were more about soldiers traveling out, locating opponents and knowing those who could be killed, or injured. It was all about making sure enemies were not able to be able to return to battle, in addition to deceit and tactics.

If the use of strategic warfare was more prevalent, then the horse that defeated the Trojans around 1180 B.C. might not be a problem. It's true that Homer is fictional and a epic, mythic poem it is possible that an individual leader, warrior or a member of the royal assembly might have suggested burning the horse. Don't "dare bring it into the gate."

What could the past be like in the event that the horse did not make it to Troy? What could happen if Trojans were aware enough that they were Greeks had been trying a final strategy before going home defeated?

One thing is that we are not fan of the Trojan horse being used as a weapon during the conflict. It could have been past five hundred years after the end of 5th century B.C. for the same deceit strategies and strategies for war to be thought of. It is also possible that the events could be the same but with one major distinction. The Trojans were the victor in that fight in place of the Greeks.

It's easy to imagine the Trojans were stoking their cups and weapons in celebration to prove that they didn't fall for the scheme, only to turn around to try and find a more effective method if they hadn't seen their defeat.

The Trojans could very likely burned the horse along with the Greeks within. Why did they bring the horse to the city?

It could be due to the manner in which the war was being fought in time time. A second reason could be pride. There was pride. Greek ships had absent. They gave a gift to be a peace offer as it seemed. It was a joy to cheer that conflict was finished and that the Greeks had been defeated would be much more enjoyable than having being concerned about traps that could be in the future.

How would it have been if Trojans were able to survive that battle? From all indications, Troy was rebuilt a several times over the years, including when Troy's "Greatest" Trojans. One could argue that the destiny of the Trojans was that they would die and that it was either around 1180 B.C. or as early as the year 500 A.D.

A different earthquake or attack occurred in a different city situated on over Troy. A mysterious cause ended it at least a couple of times. So whom or what is the one to suggest that Troy would not have been destroyed by an opponent who ended it in the same manner?

It's impossible to change the past. The Trojans that Homer imagined scattered and died after the city was taken over with The Mycenaean Greeks. They Mycenaean Greeks didn't survive much more than that. Then, there were various civilizations started, but have ended.

Nowadays, there are people living in Turkey. Troy, once the most opulent city in Troy is now a 75-acre excavation site, which is currently being excavated to find knowledge We also have flights to trade with the world. Civilizations are bound to continue and disappear. The advancement of human understanding as well as technology and fields will be continued.

However, there's one item that will stay in the past for eternity: the Trojan horse and the significance it brought for later wars. There is no question about how long it was the Trojan War occurred in ten years or one hundred.

## Chapter 13: The Impact The Trojan Horse Created

Homer used the knowledge from his experiences during the Trojan War and wrote two epic poetry. The historians aren't even able to agree as to when he was born. There is a belief that his birth date was in 1200 B.C. Some believe it's more likely that he died during the eighth century B.C. In general, the majority of scholars believe that Homer was alive about 400 years or more after when the Trojan War took place.

The poetry's dating is basing them on specific facts regarding historical events that occurred. A lot of people believe that Homer utilized wars before his time during the Trojan War and after to tell his story. Homer wasn't mention until eighth Century B.C. in the texts of historical sources.

The fact is that the Trojan horse was a significant factor regardless of Troy VIIa was destroyed by the Greeks and their deceit. Without a narrative which would entice listeners as well as readers The Trojan horse may have gone to the bottom of history, not to be remembered.

It's because of the Iliad as well as the Odyssey and other works transcending time that numerous cultures know about that of the Trojan War, the use of the Trojan horse, and also the ending of a once-large city.

The fifth century B.C., Sun Tzu published The Art of War. It was the first military reference for war planning. His precepts aid in helping Asian armies win amazing battles. However, one must ask what would Sun Tzu have come up some of these ideas with out his knowledge of the Trojan horse? Perhaps, it's just an in-depth look at the extent to which the Iliad and the other Trojan War tales traveled, nevertheless, the Trojan horse was a major effect on how the wars were waged in Asia Minor and later on.

Today, the simple concept that is the Trojan horse can be seen in some circumstances, even though it's the horse is a different model, the same concepts are still used. In the event you look at the idea of military personnel coming into the dark to take down the enemy dates all the way back to the time that it was the Trojan horse was being used.

Archeological Impact

It's not only on how the war may have changed, and indeed did when the legend of the Trojan horse traveled all over the globe. It's also about archeology. Archeologists from all over the world have spent endless hours digging for Troy. They have dug and dug until they discovered

Troy VIIa. Archeologists from the same group have been working to discover the same texts as well as oral and written evidence and other artifacts which prove that the Trojan conflict took place, and the Trojan horse had as glamorous an ending to the Trojan civilisation as Homer claimed it to be.

It is still difficult to discover the truth about the conflict. A lot of people still make pictures and television shows that share their ideas about what took place along with evidence that supports it. The writers of the past read through a variety of sources, go to the website and try to talk about how the Trojan War and the way in which they came to the conclusion that Trojan horse let the end of a decade-long or even longer war.

The Trojan horse as a strategy is a topic that is of interest to us. It's impossible to help but look for answers. In simple terms, the conflict was either caused by the presence of a woman, or the place of Troy and the fear that the Greeks had.

It was fought like any other war at this time and until some or all of the smart Mycenaean Greek warriors came up using to use the Trojan horse to completely destroy the Trojans.

## Chapter 14: The Trojans Lived, Weakened Perhaps

Homer said that the heroes that helped the Greek to return to home. The Trojans became a lost people. It is known that Troy was rebuilt. It wasn't just an urban area of Greeks when the city was rebuilt. Maybe it was because the Greeks abandoned their desire for to live in the city, or perhaps they were unable to hold on to it when the demise of their city began at the beginning.

People who were born in Troy VIIb1 to VIIb3, may have been the descendants of the Trojans that perished during The Trojan War. There is a good chance that a parts of their DNA are still due to an Etruscan connection.

Though the Homer's Trojans were utterly destroyed and completely wiped out of the earth but the truth is that a portion of them live through the descendants who remain although the blood has been diluted many times over.

Similar to the Romans that gained power later It is also possible that the Trojan warriors were held in slavery, if not those who survived during the conflict. There is a possibility that the women from Troy had become wives of Greek husbands and maintained in a nomadic lifestyle until it was the Mycenaean Greeks fell from power and moved to refugee camps.

Some may have returned to the town they used to know when it became clear that the Greeks or the person who built the city wouldn't be able to kill anyone on the spot.

The lesson to be learned is that, while conflicts are waged at the time of historical events as it comes to an end, or a civilisation ceases or is transformed into a new kind of society, wars fought might not be of significance in the thousands of years.

Consider how long it took us to find out the truth behind this Trojan War. It wasn't until the year 145 that we accepted to believe that the Trojan War as true history. In the past, the Trojan horse was originally thought of as an imaginary concept prior to the planks that are likely Trojan remains were discovered.

Allowing the gift to go through between your fortress walls, through the door to your house or even through the front door is most crucial. Without this lesson, the outcome could be differently. Perhaps we didn't remember to take care whenever a stranger comes near. It's possible you never thought about the risks of an everyday object to be dangerous, or certainly not in the way that we live in today.

The Trojans remain, either because of our genes, or as a result of their mistakes that they have been able to teach us. When the Trojans stumbled upon the horse and a horse, their lives as they had known them came to an end. they were gone. Trojan War or various wars were over for an hour, and then the city was reconstructed.

## Chapter 15: Origins

The Olympian gods that figure the foremost in the myths weren't the gods of ancient times neither were they the ones who created the universe. They appeared later, during battle and within the curse of.

At the start, there was Chaos. According to one version of the Creation story Night along with the Abyss were the first gods that emerged from Chaos. Their baby was a bright-winged Love. Then Gaia was born, also known as the goddess of Earth was born alongside her husband (and many believe, her son), Uranus, the Sky Father. Gaia was a host to animals and plants creatures, giants and monsters as well as gods known as Titans. Uranus was adamant about the giants and monsters as evil creatures and he shackled them. The incident was a sigh of sadness for Gaia who was a lover of her kids, and created a plan to be punished by Uranus. Gaia gathered her kids and the Titans and exhorted the Titans to revolt against their fathers and save their prisoners. The Titan Cronus defeated Uranus and slayed his son. Uranus flew away to shame and sadness while cursing his son. He also affirming that Cronus's children would one day take over the Titans and wrest control of the Titans.

Cronus considered threats to his authority seriously. He let the monsters as well as the giants behind in a prison cell as well as when his sister and wife Rhea gave him their children, He sucked them up whole. However, Rhea concealed their sixth son, Zeus, where Cronus would not be able to locate the child. After Zeus was at his peak of force, he fought Cronus and made him go through Zeus his siblings. They continued to live and strengthened. In the end, Zeus along with his brothers and the Olympians were at war with the Titans.

Through the assistance of Prometheus, the intelligent Titan Prometheus who retreated towards them, and also of giants and monsters who they rescued from their chains, the Olympians took on and kept the Titans at their own turns. After some time the peace reigned between heaven and earth. And the time of mythology's great stories started.

**Chapter 16: Gods, Goddesses And Spirits**

What were the names of the conquered gods? There are many names given to all the characters in both historical and literary accounts (see the Appendix A). The time that the Romans were able to take over the Greek city-states they adopted the mythology of those they had defeated, however they changed the names of gods and heroes using their native culture. Contemporary references could use Greek or Roman names.

The Gods and Goddesses of the world form the foundation of what's commonly referred to as The Greek Pantheon. The principal gods from the Pantheon are referred to by the name of The Twelve Olympians, residing atop Mount Olympus. It was at Mount Olympus that the Gods held court, and would take part in fierce debates. It was believed that the Ancient Greeks believed that mortals weren't allowed to pass through Olympus's gates. Olympus and believed that the peak was too tall for anyone to reach. In the great hall of council at the top of Mount Olympus, the Gods were seated at great feasts, as well as feasted on ambrosia, gin and nectar. They made choices which shaped the future of humanity and frequently interacted with everyday individuals.

Despite their eternality and heavenly powers however, the Gods were vulnerable to the same weaknesses of humankind as human beings on earth. They were constantly fighting among them and were susceptible to anger and jealousy. The actions they took were often insane and showed the weaknesses of humanity.

Zeus was the highest of Zeus was the most powerful of Olympian gods. Zeus ruled over the heavens and was the god of thunder, which was feared by men and gods. He defined and often required, the right conduct among people of the earth: reverence for gods, reverence for dead people, fidelity to oaths and vows, concern for the needy elderly, those who were sick and homeless. His behavior could be doubtful. He was cruelly punishes Prometheus in his attempt to defend the human race and to enlighten them (see Prometheus' section below). Also, he was frequently infidelity, engaging in intrigues with immortal and mortal women and attempting, often unsuccessfully to hide his affairs away from wife Hera.

Hera was Zeus Hera was Zeus' wife, sister as well as queen. Hera was also the goddess of goddesses Ares and Hephaestus along with the lesser gods Eilithya and Eilithya, who sheltered women when they were in labor, as well as Hebe she was the goddess of young people. Hera is believed to safeguard mothers. However, she was unkind to women who gave babies to Zeus. Hera was Zeus his mortal love Io imprisoned in the form of a cow. She was chased across the sea and land by a flies that had a painful bite. As Zeus was a father to children through Leto, the Titaness Leto, Hera made certain that the land she was in would not let her rest or have a child to her children there. (Eventually, Leto found a floating island, where she was able to give birth to Apollo as well as Artemis.)

Ares was the father of Zeus and Hera and god of battle. The Greeks were averse to him and the devastation he brought about with doubt. The Romans were more likely to respect the man. According to some stories, Aphrodite was his lover although not necessarily the husband of Aphrodite.

Aphrodite is the name given to her by they Romans refer to as Venus as the most gorgeous goddess of love was created when Uranus' blood Uranus was poured onto the ocean's foam. People of the world adored and revered her due to the pleasure she brought. They also saw her as the one who gave them despair, jealousy as well as despair and madness that can be the dark part of affection.

Hephaestus is Hera's child. There are stories that say Zeus was the father of Hephaestus; other stories say Hera who was suffering from Zeus's sins, fashioned Hephaestus in her own name without assistance from Zeus and gave birth to him the child of a fatherless mother. He was god's smith creating the gods' weapons and ornaments. People praised him since he taught them how to master working with metal. Gods enjoyed a more than a friendly connection to his work. He was banished from the sky, possibly due to his mother's opinion that his appearance was unattractive or Zeus disliked his joining Hera's side during a fight. He was immortal, and therefore could not be destroyed, but his falling shattered his body forever. In later years, Gods praised him for his sagacity and intelligence. He was the husband of Aphrodite however, numerous stories claim that she cheated on him by choosing the attractive Ares.

Artemis is the goddess of virginity is the goddess of Zeus and Leto. Her archery skills were legendary as well as the patron of hunterkind, and the guardian of wild animals as well as hero of the virgins, and in addition (with Hera) the protector of women in labor. According to mythology, she was associated with the goddess of moon Selene and Hecate who is the queen of the Underworld.

Apollo was Artemis his brother, and was the god of sun as well as the prophetic. Deathly souls with burning questions went to the shrine of Apollo in Delphi by bringing gifts, and the priestess to call the Oracle to provide them with the answer of Apollo. The priestess would fall in a state of trance, and then return with Apollo's words. It was always the truth because Apollo does not conceal his truth. Yet, Apollo could and did of time frame his truth in so obscure or confusing terms that respondents were lost. In other instances, as they attempted to prevent disasters from being triggered by the oracle they created those very disasters that they were afraid of (This occurs in the myth of Oedipus which is later told in this work). If we refer to Delphic comments or predictions in reference to Apollo. Apollo was also patron saint of the arts as well as was the father of Aesculapius who was who was the goddess of healing.

Athena was the goddess of full-form who emerged out of the head Zeus rather than being born as one would expect she was a virgin goddess of wisdom. She instructed humans on how to control horses, tend cattle, plant olive trees, and various other crops weave, spin and worked in clay. Her name was believed to be the goddess of war but in the Trojan War (described in detail in the future) she was on the side of the enemies. Athens was the city that she ruled. Athens was subject to her special security.

Hermes Another illegitimate son of Zeus is the god of robbery and trading. Hermes was also Zeus as messenger and spiritual guide to souls heading for the graveyard of the dead.

Poseidon, Zeus' second brother, was god of the sea and was thus a god of great importance for the people that lived in islands and on peninsulas, and conducted their trade through the sea. In times of anger, he swung the great trident, which created storms on the sea as well as earthquakes on the land. In his rage, he constructed islands, and offered safe access for vessels. He was also the inventor of horses.

Hades was Zeus the third brother of Zeus. As Zeus was in the heavens, Hades ruled over the Underworld that was the dark world of the dead. Its entry was guarded by a vicious tri-headed dog Cerberus. In the course of four months, year Hades his unfaithful wife Persephone was at his flanks. It is believed that the Ancient Greeks sometimes included Hades as well as Persephone as part of their Twelve Olympians, but in the majority of cases, they were not as they lived within the realm of the dead.

Demeter was Zeus the god's sister as well as Persephone's mother. Demeter was also goddess of earth's fertility, creator of the grain, and also the source to drive every growth. In the time that Hades kidnapped Persephone, Demeter abandoned her love for earth, while she searched for her daughter all over the world. When winter came to the earth and the plants perished in the fields and animals and humans were hungry. Zeus demanded that Hades return his bride. what he was able to achieve was a bargained agreement. After that, for four years every year Persephone resided together with Hades, Demeter mourned and the plants perished, however during the eight months of each year Persephone as well as life went back to the realm above the earth. According to some stories, Demeter may also be the maternal grandmother of Dionysus.

Dionysus is the goddess of wine as well as of fertility. The god was blamed for ecstasy and for the craziness of his people and for the arts of drama. Death and rebirth of him similar to Persephone's death celebrations were held as the season changed.

## Other Important Deities

Eros who is known to us through his Latin name, Cupid (though the word "erotic is derived out of Eros' Greek name) is the son of Aphrodite. Eros shot his arrows with magic towards gods and people who were struck by the shafts of his bow fell completely and in love with. The pain that would result of this resulted in a variety of tales. There were those who claimed the boy was willful shooting his arrows randomly, while others claimed claim that he was blindfolded and blind. In one instance, as per Apulueius'[1] story about Cupid and Psyche the king hit himself with one his own arrows. He then, after many years of sharing joy and sorrow discovered how wonderful and terrifying it was to be loved.

Proteus is the name given to him by his son or possibly the servant of Poseidon. He was very wise and mythological characters seeking answers to questions of the moment often looked to him rather than Apollo's oracle. His words were more cryptic than the ones from the oracle. However, they were also more difficult to be found. Anyone who needed answers from him would have be able to hold the man. This wasn't an easy job because he had the ability to transform his body whenever he wanted to; when he was seized by him, he could take on the appearance of a variety of monsters in quick sequence, as well as tiny soft creatures which can easily flee. People who were strong and courageous enough to remain with the man in his various forms were eventually rewarded with his wise advice. It is still common to refer to highly changing situations, or individuals that are Protean as well as The Protean

Charm that is featured in Harry Potter books. Harry Potter books also originates from Proteus.

Prometheus which also signifies Forethought and Forethought, wasn't an Olympian however, he was the word means Titan and a member of the old Gods race. He aided the Olympians in their rebellion against the oppressive rule of the Titans and for an time it was possible for him to rule alongside the Olympians. However, he was still able to help those who were weak and new. Many writers believe they believe it was Prometheus (with some aid by his twin brother Epimetheus who's name is an etymological reference to the Greek word meaning "afterthought") and created the human race as well as gave them the wisdom of desire for greater understanding. The innate curiosity and thirst for knowledge led mankind to be near to gods.

Prometheus made the threat even more dangerous by taking fire from the heavens and distributing it to people for warmth, light as well as defense, and for craftsmanship. The Olympians were not able to destroy the human race They were not able to remove Prometheus gift away but they could punish the person who gave them. In the beginning, Zeus tied Prometheus to the top of a mountain in which an Eagle (Zeus bird) attacked his liver each day (it was regrown every night; Prometheus was not able to escape the ashes in the case of Prometheus). If he refused to bow down to Zeus and even complain about Zeus unfair treatment to everyone that passed by, he was thrown in the hell of the dead forever.

The Muses were the nine daughters of Titaness Mnemosyne the goddess of memories. They brought happiness, inspiration and creativity. Certain stories deal with them in a collective way and others provide them with their own name and specifics.

The Erinyes (also known as Furies are far stronger beings. They were made of blood from Cronus. They were avenging the perpetrators of crime specifically murder. They pursued their victims with relentless force and often drove them into the brink of despair and madness. However, when they pursued Orestes the goddess who murdered his mother as a retribution to her murder of his father He was able to bear the complete terror of what he'd done, and at the time declared that he was making the right decision to make, and then they agreed to let him go and leave at peace. There are stories that say that following the change in their character, they transformed and they were renamed the Eumenides or the

Mercies however in other tales, they still haunt all over the world.

The Moirae The Moirae, also known as Fates were also awful and in a detached way. At birth, they gave each person their time to be good or evil. Clotho was spinning the life-line, Lachesis determined the length then Atropos took it and cut the thread. (Our term 'atropine' comes directly from the woman.)

## Chapter 17: Short Tales Of Gods And Heroes

A lot of the common speech figures originate from the stories that are part of Greek mythology. Many of these stories remain retold completely in our society. Some have diminished in popularity to time however, they have traces of their existence in our daily speech. The tales that led to these characters of speech include a variety of explanations for the world of nature as well as the travels of mythological characters within a world controlled by Gods. They have remained within the English vocabulary for many years and stood the tests of time.

Pandora's Box:

Asking innocent questions, which reveal disturbing truths, or initiate movements that have unexpected outcomes is often believed as having opened Pandora's Box. However, none of these actions has as profound an impact such as opening the first box of the story of Hesiod. [2]

It is possible to recall from earlier in this section the story of Prometheus The creator of all mankind. He took the fire of Mount Olympus and gave it humans to use for security, warmth, as well as works of art. Prometheus together with his solitary brother Epimetheus was instrumental in the creation of species on Earth and entrusted the creatures with a variety of qualities. After Zeus realized that humankind had acquired fire, he became angry. Prometheus was punished severely for stealing, but before being taken to be held in captivity, he warned Epimetheus not to accept any offer from Zeus. Epimetheus accepted the warning and then promptly did not remember. Then, when Zeus created a gorgeous woman, gave her the name of Pandora and proposed her to Epimetheus to marry,

Epimetheus accepted with delight. Zeus also presented a present to Pandora with a gift box, which was instructed by him to not unpack. Pandora was adamant, however with time her curiosity increased. What was in the box? How did it get there to her, even if she would never access it? The lid was raised only a bit to look in...and there came out a multitude of winged creatures. But before she had the chance to slam it down, they were all released to the sky. They were mostly evil creatures, suffering from sickness and sorrows of all sorts Some even say death is the ultimate cause. However, there was a beautiful spirit who flew alongside them: Elpis the name of which in English is Hope and who gave people the strength to face every evil that went to the outside world with her.

Sowing the Dragon's Teeth:

The term is employed for all events that lead to long-running disputes. The symbolic "sowing" of dragon's teeth occurred twice in Greek mythologies. The first century poet Apollodorus said that Apollo promises Cadmus who was the fabled creator of Thebes to eventually build and run the city. Apollo advised Cadmus which city location would be situated. Cadmus took the advice of Apollo but was shocked to discover the site of the city guarded by the ferocious dragon. Following a frenzied battle, Cadmus managed to kill the dragon. As he was beginning to think about whom he could ask for help to create his own town, Athena told him to put in the teeth of the deceased dragon. He followed through and was frightened by the sight of a group of Armed and clearly fierce warriors appeared out of the ground. It was fortunate that they fought each other and not Cadmus fighting until they were all killed. Five exhausted men lay down their weapons, and decided to cooperate peacefully with each other and to serve Cadmus.

The second time as per the third century Greek poet Apollonius his heroic Jason had been sent out to steal the Golden Fleece from a foreign monarch to obtain his claim to the kingdom which previously been the property of his grandfather. Aetes was the king who retained the Fleece was in agreement with the conditions that Jason must plough the field using two fierce bulls as well as plant dragon's tooth within the furrows and take care of the crops which grew out of them. Aetes his granddaughter, Medea, gave Jason the magic charm which let him control the bulls and advised Jason that once the warriors sprouted out of the dragon's teeth, Jason had to throw a stone to make them fight each other. The boy followed her suggestion and fought through.

The Golden Touch:

We say today that a person is blessed with the golden touch when they demonstrate exceptional skills or luck. The original Golden Touch was a very risky offer.

According to the story of Ovid the king Midas from Phrygia once performed a favor to Dionysus god of wine and the giver of hazardous gifts, by giving to him an adored fan who got lost in a stupor of alcohol. Dionysus was thankful and promised to grant Midas whatever he wanted. Midas wanted that anything touched by him would change to gold. The request was fulfilled in a short time moment Midas entertained himself by turning the flowers of his garden into incredible bronze sculptures. When he finally sat down for dinner, he realized the gardener had made a huge wrong. Each bite of food, every glass of wine changed to gold when it touched the lips or hands He soon realised that he was likely to die from hunger if the gods did not give him back his prize. He was fortunate that Dionysus showed mercy to him and took away the Golden Touch away.

## Chapter 18: Flying Too High

The famous inventor Daedalus was perhaps the smartest man in his time. In the end, his inventions brought him into the spotlight of the ruthless King Minos.

Minos one time took his son on a trip to Athenians. While in Athens the young man participated in a hazardous adventure and was killed. With rage and grief Minos took over Athens and threatened dismantle the city and murder all of the inhabitants of it unless they offer him a tribute consisting comprising seven men and seven females each year. They were in agreement. Minos took over Daedalus and ordered him to devise the difficult maze, which is known as the Labyrinth. The Labyrinth turned into the home of the monster that is half-bull, half-human known as the Minotaur. The Labyrinth also served as the place of execution for Athenian young people who were confined to walk around in blindness until the Minotaur was able to find them.

However, Daedalus was a gentle man who was grieving over what he was made to be forced to. He learned that the daughter of King Ariadne was also a fan of Athenians, Daedalus told her there was a method for them to avoid the Labyrinth. You just need to take one ball of thread and put it into the entrance and let it unwind behind them while they walk the pathways through the Labyrinth.

As the following group of homages arrived, Ariadne fell in love with a young man who was enslaved called Theseus who gave him the thread ball that was also known as the clue. Theseus was lucky enough to discover the Minotaur asleep and then kill the creature. After that, he and his fellow followers followed the trail back to the gate, and took Ariadne along with them, and then fled towards Athens.

Minos discovered the fact that Daedalus was the one who had aided in the escape of his friends, and was furious and imprisoned Daedalus as well as his son Icarus at the heart of the emptied Labyrinth. Daedalus himself was unable to trace the path of the maze that he created. He realised there was an alternative way out. He created wings for him and his son made of feathers and wax, and then they flew to the high point of the Labyrinth's walls before preparing to fly across the ocean towards Sicily. Daedalus advised his son not to fly at a low altitude, as the waves could drag him to the bottom or fly too high in the case of a sun that could cause his wings to melt. However, Icarus was enthralled by the joy of flying and could not keep from circling upwards in the sky until his wings became melted, and he fell into the ocean.

## Chapter 19: The Complex Tale Of Oedipus And The Self-Fulfilling Prophecies

Freud's theory about his theory of the Oedipus complex, the boys are possessed by an unrequited sexual attraction to their mothers, and the desire to be rid of their fathers is fairly well known. But the original Oedipus, in Sophocles' tragedy Oedipus Rex, was trying his hardest--consciously, at least--to avoid killing his father and marrying his mother. The causes of his demise are...well complicated.

The story starts with Oedipus his parents the The king Laius as well as the queen Jocasta of Thebes and Apollo's oracle in Delphi regarding the baby Jocasta was to bear. The oracle advised that Jocasta's child could someday take his father's life. Laius determined that this event would never occur, and took action swiftly and brutally to avoid this from happening.

When Jocasta was born to her baby son, Laius tied the baby's feet tightly together and handed the baby to a shepherd instructing the shepherd to take his baby in the wild. Laius believed that this will remove him from any dangers that his son posed but without causing bloodguilt or God's punishment.

However, the shepherd was kind to the child, and didn't leave the child. He travelled far beyond Laius the kingdom, and handed the child to a different shepherd to rear. The shepherd didn't even explain where the child was from. The shepherd who was second in line, compassionate, knew the rulers of his family and kings, King Polybus and Queen Merope of Corinth had no children and wanted an successor. The boy was brought to them and they welcomed the baby, and named the boy Oedipus (which refers to'swollen feet," since the bindings were causing ankle pain) He was loved by them as an infant son.

Oedipus developed into a powerful confident, intelligent and bold young man. He seemed content until the day a drunk threw a punch at Oedipus, claiming he was not the son of his father. Oedipus was furious, he went to the oracle in Delphi and inquired whether he was related to his father. The oracle said that he would be cursed with the destiny of killing his father and get married to his mother. Oedipus terrified, he ran away from the land.

In the course of his journey, the driver came across a crossing. A man of old age riding in a car was crossing the road, accompanied by four attendants. He yelled at Oedipus to move out of the way. However, when Oedipus was not moving fast enough to accommodate him, he made the driver of his carriage push

Oedipus into the way. Oedipus was a king and isn't used to being pulled around. He slammed the man on the back of his car with his full force. The man didn't want that it was a fatal strike, but it did happen. The servants fought Oedipus afterward the king killed three of them. Just one of them fled from the scene.

Oedipus continued to travel, but without a clear goal seeking to be away from King Polybus as well as Queen Merope in order to not cause harm to the two queens. As he learned that The town of Thebes was under attack by a colossal beast, Oedipus turned his attention towards the west, believing it was either his choice to fight the beast to protect the city, or go to die courageously, without hurting his adoptive parents.

The animal that was in question was called the Sphinx which was a huge male lion, with wings and a woman's face. The

Sphinx was seated outside the gates of Thebes and was able to snare those who attempted to get into Thebes. She allowed her victims to leave if they could answer the question correctly. However, until now, no one has discovered the right answer. she was able to kill them all. They were locked up and were running low on food.

After Oedipus offered the correct answer, the Sphinx committed suicide in her anger And the happy Thebans declared Oedipus King, as their King, Laius, was newly gone, with no children. Oedipus got married to the Queen who had died and then ruled alongside her as well as her sister Creon. They had two sons as well as two daughters. For some time Thebes was prosperous and peaceful.

Then, the plague hit. The fields were swollen with rot Grapes and olive trees dropped decaying fruit and cows miscarried. The babies born at Thebes weren't born while a degenerative disease quickly spread killing old and young alike. The Thebans called out to Oedipus to protect them from the plague just like he helped them escape the Sphinx. Oedipus went back to the oracle of Apollo and sent a messenger to inquire about what they needed to take to get rid of the plague. The result was with the following message: King Laius died and must be brought to justice, and the person who did it exiled.

Oedipus who arrived just after Laius had died, asked about what been the fate of the King, and in the event that he was killed, his murder had not been swiftly avenged. The people were able to explain they believed that Laius was killed by robbers when he was traveling away from Thebes and the Sphinx's attack had occurred shortly following his death that they were left with no time to consider or confront his murderers. Oedipus was furious at them for not being in their duties, and declared a curse upon Laius the murderer, and then began to investigate with the prophet blind Tiresias to inquire whether his second sight could shed light on the circumstances surrounding Laius.

Tiresias was once dissected the fetched, was extremely reticent to discuss the meaning of anything. Oedipus accused him of the duty he owed to his country Then he proceeded with personal allegations and threats. Tiresias was furious and claimed the blame was Oedipus who killed Laius. Oedipus was furious and denied the claim and accusing Tiresias of lying to undermine him. He also claimed that Queen Jocasta's brother Creon of provoking the prophet to fight Oedipus in order to ensure that Creon could be crowned King. Jocasta attempted to reconcile with her husband by saying that Creon was committed to him, and that prophets and prophecies are inherently not reliable. What was the reason, she had said that her son would murder his father. However, this had never occurred; Laius had been murdered by robbers in the first place, the point in which three roads intersected.

This assurance frightened Oedipus. He inquired of Jocasta about what Laius was like. The description she gave was similar to Oedipus his memory of the old, arrogant man he killed at the crossing. He was still wrestling with the issue when a messenger walked up to his aid from Corinth and informed him that King Polybus was dead--of natural and old age-- and the inhabitants of Corinth were waiting for Oedipus to come back and reign in their place.

Oedipus expressed gratitude to God for saving his father from killing him as per the prophecy, which drove him out of Corinth however, he also said it was impossible to go back as the queen Merope continued to live and he feared it would be his fate to get being married to her. The messenger was confused. After Oedipus was able to repeat the prophecy the messenger informed him that it was not necessary to be worried about going back to Corinth because Merope wasn't Oedipus mom nor related to Oedipus. Oedipus inquired about how this could have happened as the messenger identified him as the Shepherd who taken Oedipus as a child abandoned and brought him to the Queen and King. In response to questions, the shepherd claimed that he'd taken the child from the Theban shepherd. Oedipus summoned the shepherd. The man who responded to the summons was unable to give Oedipus any information, however Oedipus threatened him with his death. After that, the shepherd told him that he had obtained Oedipus to the King Creon as well as Queen Jocasta which had left him to die and had saved the man out of compassion.

Oedipus discovered with awe that he too, as Laius were trying to avoid their fates. He realized that these efforts brought their destiny to pass. He pleaded with the Thebans to murder him because the fact that he was unable to bear the guilt. The family declined. Jocasta killed herself. Oedipus was blinded, but was still begging for his death however, Creon exiled him instead.

Gods showed a sort of compassion for Oedipus at the end of the day by bringing the man to an safe shelter and letting know that the location in which he passed peacefully be blessed for his merits. The curse was awaited Oedipus's children.

Sons Oedipus' became involved in murderous rivalries, while his courageous and pious daughter Antigone was executed in pity for her brother that was defeated. The subsequent history of Oedipus and his family is revealed in Sophocles his plays Oedipus and Antigone at Colonus and Antigone as well as in Aeschylus the The Seven Against Thebes. The Seven Against Thebes.

### Chapter 20: The Trojan War

The conflict between Greeks along with The Trojans was the topic of Homer's epic poem The Iliad. Much like many of the human conflicts in Greek legend, this one started with a war between gods.

Eris is the goddess of discord wasn't very well-liked either in the eyes of gods and people. There was once a huge gathering to which she as the only god wasn't invited. She was angry and determined to make the rest of us equally miserable as she had been. The goddess made a stunning golden apple that she wrote on "For the most fair," and threw it in the hall of banquets with gods. Each goddess promptly demanded the apple to herself. A few later agreed, or even forced to drop their claims. Three remain unconvinced: Hera, Aphrodite, and Athena. They pleaded with Zeus to decide among them. Zeus shrewdly declined and suggested instead to take the advice of the king Paris of Troy who was an eminent lover of beauty.

The goddesses immediately came out, and demanded to be invited to Paris. Each of them offered a substantial reward for being deemed the most beautiful. Hera offered to create Paris the supreme ruler of Europe as well as Asia. Athena stated that she would command a victorious army in order to defeat Greece. Aphrodite assured him of the most gorgeous woman on earth. Paris was more attracted to women than fighting was enticed by Aphrodite's proposal.

It was a simple issue. The most gorgeous woman on earth is undoubtedly Helen was the child of Zeus and mortal women. Helen had already been wed to Menelaus King of Sparta. At the time that Helen was not yet married, every prince of Greece were looking for her to marry, and her father given them the promise that, if she was kidnapped after the wedding, her old lovers would unite against the kidnapper. When Paris arrived in Sparta as a prestigious guest and observed Helen and her family, he did not care about the risk. He was alongside the couple until they all believed in him. Later the moment Menelaus went on a trip, Paris stole Helen away.

Menelaus as well as the armies of Greek Kingmen who were the lovers of Helen were in hot chase, but by the time their ships arrived in the Trojan territories, Paris and his stolen bride were safe inside the fortified city of Troy The Trojan troops were ready to protect their position. Over the course of nine years, the war was fought back and forth. Both sides had what believed was a legitimate motive. The Greeks wanted to avenge a break of the sacred bond of marriage as well as hospitality. The Trojans were protecting their capital against an armed opponent who could take brutal and unjustified to take revenge. Both, at some moment, believed they were fighting for their honour.

In order to make matters more difficult to make things more complicated, for the sake of complication, Olympians often intervened from both side. Aphrodite continued to be interested in fighting for Paris due to evident reasons. Her love interest Ares was also involved; also Apollo as well as Artemis. Hera and Athena were both on their Greek side. They both were deemed less attractive by Paris and wanted to show him regret for the decision. Hera had a tendency to feel sympathy to spouses who were wronged. Athena was a fan of the Greek camp. Odysseus the wisest and most clever of all

Greeks. Poseidon was also a part of the group.

Hector is the best combatant of the Trojans Hector, who was adamantly disapproving of Paris's actions but felt obliged to protect his countrymen played a significant role in the war. The war ended when the Greeks most formidable fighter, Achilles, quarreled bitterly with his king Agamemnon who took the concubine of Achilles the wife. Achilles believed that this was an act of vengeance and was unwilling fighting to win the woman of another under the guidance of a man who stripped him of his own. He walked out of the fight. This was a great loss to the Greeks, for Achilles was bold, strong and skilled in battle, and also--very nearly--invulnerable. While he was an infant baby the mother of his Thetis would have dipped him into the holy Styx river Styx to guard him from serious injuries. The touching of the water had as much effect as Thetis was hoping. However, she was unaware that there was an area of him that the water had didn't touch: his heel, the way she held the man in the water.

The Trojans inspired by Achilles his absence, launched to attack the Greeks and killed a lot of them, and drove survivors to their boats. Achilles"my dear friend" Patroclus who was weaker and less angry man, begged Achilles to save his family. Achilles, still furious, refused. Patroclus was able to borrow Achilles his distinctive armor, sported it, and fought alongside him and promised Achilles that he'd help save Achilles' Greek troops from destruction and not launch an attack. The Trojans were convinced that Achilles was a threat but they retreated in terror; the Greeks chased them to as long as the wall of Troy. Patroclus took on their heads in a state of forgetting his pledge. However, when Hector began to take on the Greek champion Hector defeated Patroclus quickly, only to realize later that it wasn't Achilles that was dead in front of Hector.

Achilles in a state of sadness and sorrow, opted to take on his fellow Greeks to battle. Hector in fear for his own people and sick of the massacre, demanded an end to the fight and called Achilles to a single battle, requesting that only the winner was to be buried with honor. Achilles declined the challenge however, but he agreed to the challenge being aware that Athena was adamant to help his strength and weaken Hector. When the fight was over, Hector recognized that he was facing far more than mortals, however, he refused to surrender. He was killed in battle, and Achilles saw his body carried around the city on horses however, after Priam the king of Troy and the father of Hector arrived without arms and pleaded for the son's remains, Achilles gave it to Hector, and the two struck an end to the war as the Trojans were buried and mourned over their fallen hero.

In the aftermath of the truce after the truce, however, the Trojans were more ferocious than they had ever before in the midst of their sorrow and anger. Then they Greeks had lost their champion; Paris laid an ambush and killed Achilles at the sole weak point of his body, his heel. The war seemed to be one that could never be over and at the very least, it would not end until all soldiers were killed.

Odysseus the smartest of Athena's favorite determined that the win was to be won through fraud, not force. He revealed his plans to his friends. Then, the Trojans awakened to discover that they had discovered that the Greek ships had gone away. The place where was the Greek camps had been, there was only one man in fear and a huge wooden horse.

The man claimed that the Greeks were depressed about their the victory and fled however, they planned to first kill him as a sacrifice for humanity in order to guarantee their safe return home. He left, and was no longer loyal to Greece. He further explained to them that the wooden horse was a sacrifice that the Greeks left behind in order in order to please the gods they obviously had upset. Naturally, it could be a blessing for the Greeks in the event that it were left at the site of their camp. If it was brought to the city of Troy and bestowed blessings on the Trojans However, the Greeks were skeptical that they could trust that the Trojans were thinking of this...

The Trojans were ruled by prophets who advised that they should not believe in the Greeks or to ride horses; later Latin poet

Aeneas expressed the message in the form of "Beware of Greeks with gifts" which is a phrase we listen to even today. However, the Trojan population did not listen at their gods (Not reading prophecies within the Greek mythology, is thought to be just as harmful as reading the words of their prophets). They brought their horse inside their walls and the next day, they ate and were awed.

The next night, the Greek soldiers who were hidden within the horse, descended through a concealed trapdoor and climbed out, then took on at the sleeping city. Disappointed by the conflict and the huge losses as well, the Greeks ignored both their compassion for the common people and respect to the gods. The king who was aging Priam was killed before an altar dedicated to Zeus as was his daughter Cassandra, the goddess of prophecy who had advised the Trojans to destroy their wooden horse was taken by Athena's altar and raped and forced into the shackles of. In the following day, the entire population of Troy were dead or committed to a life of slaves in Greece.

## Chapter 21: The Odyssey

The gods, including ones who had favoured the Greeks and were furious over the savage sacking of Troy. Athena who was the protector Cassandra tried to find but failed sought, visited Poseidon the god of sea, and begged Poseidon to create the storm to disperse the Greek ship as they headed to home. The god was eager to help. The Greeks exuberant with their triumph but unprepared to withstand the raging storm, which hit them when they were middle-ocean and had no shelter. Ajax the Cassandra's slayer, was drowned. Agamemnon's ships were scattered, and several of them were lost. Agamemnon eventually sailed back to his home and was killed by his wife and the man she had met in her absence. The longest return journey was the one of Odysseus. The epic poem of Homer The Odyssey describes that voyage as well as defining our modern term for epic travel.

Odysseus was a ship that survived the storm, however when the sea calmed down, the ship was still in uncharted waters. The remainder of the Greek fleet could not be found, and the captain didn't know which route to navigate to find the home he had made in Ithaca and his wife Penelope as well as his son Telemachus which was just a baby at the time Odysseus left for the conflict.

The very first place Odysseus and his sailors traveled to appeared friendly. People welcomed them with warmth and presented them with sweet-smelling floral arrangements to eat. Odysseus and the rest of his crew were skeptical of the unusual meals. Some ate then declared immediately the trip was finished and they'd found the most delicious country on earth and were not interested in finding alternative country to call home. Odysseus in a state of panic, warned the rest of his soldiers to take the offerings from the people who ate Lotus. He took the people who ate the bouquets back to their ship, and tied them up as they wept. They wanted only to smell the bouquets again.

In the next island, they discovered a vast cave where the proprietor had left from the island. Odysseus and his hungry companions consumed the food set out and were ready to serve wines from the ship's store after their host had returned. Their host was revealed to be not a mere mortal and was a gigantic, single-eyed Cyclops called Polyphemus. He wasn't impressed with the wine offer, nor was he impressed by Odysseus' claim that his men were under security of Zeus and that he was watching over the guests and even beggars. The king disarmed all of them and secluded them from the cave by imposing rock, and then ate two men, and assured them that no one would ever escape his home alive. On the following day Polyphemus killed another two individuals and then left his cave to care for his flock of sheep. In search of a way to make a profit, Odysseus and his men constructed a huge spear taking down wood from the walls, then putting it with the help of a fire. Then, when Polyphemus came back, Odysseus got him drunk and then shut his eye out. On the next day, Polyphemus led his animals out to graze however, unable to discern the sheep, he tried to touch the backs of his sheep in case they were attempting to escape. However, Odysseus and his companions put themselves in the belly of the animals as they left the cave, and returned to their boat.

They seemed safe in the present However, they'd screamed to end the hatred of Poseidon because Polyphemus was the son of Poseidon. Poseidon swears in rage that Odysseus will find his house as well as his family after his entire army was dead and he was himself been wandering in a state of despair for a lengthy time. Poseidon did not break his word.

It was some time following this, Odysseus landed on an island with the same beauty as that from the Lotus eaters. He arranged for a small group to explore the area. The beautiful lady named Circe was gracious enough to invite them inside and served the group wines to consume. The majority, if not one consumed the wine and immediately changed to porcines. The man who escaped was the last to inform Odysseus the story of what happened.

Odysseus instructed the person to return aboard the ship and to keep the rest of the crew there in the meantime Odysseus set out on his own to help his lost men.

Hermes was moved by Odysseus the brave, handed the man a magic herb that made him impervious to all the poisons of Circe. Odysseus consumed her drink and kept his shape and demanded her to free his soldiers. Circe was awestruck, and brought them back to their normal shape and seated him with his crew for the duration of a time while they dealt with injuries and grievances. The alcohol she fed them during in that time was quite safe. She then used her magical skills to inform Odysseus about the dangers which would await him as he headed to home.

The most enigmatic of the dangers was Siren Song. Sirens sang. Sirens had immortal ladies that performed so well that audience lost all thought except for the music. They sang to the music with awe until they passed away from hunger and thirst. Circe encouraged Odysseus and his crew to put their ears in when they got close to the rocks on which the Sirens were singing. Odysseus was a follower of the advice to his men, however was keen to hear the songs. His crew was instructed to attach him to the mast and pledge not to let him go until they had gotten past the threat of the music. They did as he asked. The music was hypnotic indeed as were the words that the Sirens performed were more appealing to the fast-thinking Odysseus. The Sirens sang that all knowledge and every secret was theirs and that the person who came before them would discover everything... Odysseus begged the group to release him However, his plea for mercy did not go down well and the threat was safely passed.

The second danger was simple and more difficult to avoid. It was a way to home that took you to a narrow passageway between two dangers: Scylla, a six-headed sea monster and Charybdis an enormous whirlpool that was enough to sink any vessel. However, even Odysseus one of the most skilled mariners be unable to avoid these dangers. Odysseus instructed them to move closer to Scylla and another six people died, however the ship sailed on to calmer waters. From there, it went towards an island in the Sun. There, Odysseus advised his crew not to harm or touch any living thing; after that, the king went off in solitude to chant prayers. On his return, he saw that the crew of his hungry men were eating and killing the sacred Sun's Oxen. The crew fled their vessel and a second storm, avenging on the victims of the Oxen, hit and sank the ship. The men in the crew drowned

However, Odysseus was found dead on the beach of a different island.

This island was the residence of the lovely Nymph Calypso. She helped heal and fed Odysseus she welcomed him to her island as well as to her bedroom, and provided all the things he could want, with the thing he had always wanted most of all: a boat that could transport the man home to Ithaca. It was an oasis soon began to be a place of confinement. It was a matter of time before days became months, weeks became years. Odysseus became sick of the desire to return the comforts of home.

Poseidon is still angry with Odysseus for the reason of Polyphemus However, other Olympians began to feel sorry for Odysseus and feel Odysseus had paid the full price for his role in the demise of Troy. Athena particularly wanted to aid her loved one who was clever. Athena waited until Poseidon got caught up in his own personal affairs, and later convinced the other Olympians to unite to help bring Odysseus back home. Hermes instructed Calypso to build the raft that Odysseus to return home on And Athena carried him across the ocean to Ithaca.

However, his troubles didn't end with the death of his wife. His wife Penelope wanted and was waiting for him, however many of the wealthy and powerful men living nearby believed that Odysseus was dead and his wife as well as the land he owned were his to be taken. They poured into Penelope's home and slapped her with constant suggestions. They didn't want to stir anyone to anger by refusing to marry them. Instead, she informed them that she was not allowed to marry until she was finished with an extravagant shroud to honor her deceased husband, in case the man was actually dead. She was working in the shroud each day. It took them a bit of time to realise that she was taking her work home at the night. When they realized that the situation was getting more aggressive. They continued to stay in the palace, merrily and destroying things, soaking to Odysseus items, scolding his servants and daughters, inflicting insults on his son Telemachus and affirming that they would not quit until Penelope decided to accept one. Each day, she discovered different reasons to delay her selection. Every day, the suitors became more irritable. In the event that Telemachus became older enough to be an actual threat to the group, they were planning to kill him however, Athena protected him by hiding him and keeping the man safe. Penelope became abandoned and became was becoming increasingly anxious.

The situation was as it was at the time Odysseus arrived at Ithaca's shores tired and isolated. Athena approached his aid and informed him to not go home in a public manner and that his bride's lovers could be able to kill him. He was able to find a safe place close to the palace. She took Telemachus to the palace, and assisted them in forming an idea.

The next day, a unruly beggar walked into the palace, asking for a place to stay. The guests were a bit sarcastic about him and one even slapped the beggar. Penelope was upset by this act of hostility. The beggar was yelled at by her, showed him respect and respect, and then asked him in private where he came from. He told him a pathetic tale of meeting Odysseus during his travels and Penelope began to cry until the man was astonished. The suitors were either too drunk, or in pondering the meaning of what Penelope told the stranger, to be aware the weapons were hidden from sight.

On the next day, lovers were more insistent than they had ever been. Penelope stated she'd marry the one who was able to string and precisely shoot the huge bow Odysseus left behind when the ship went off for war. Each man attempted and did not succeed. The ragged beggar finally was ready to make his move. He was mocked by his suitors however he fired the archer through the object after which Athena removed his mask and appeared before the crowd in his personal form, with the appearance of Odysseus. No one left this place alive, however there was a great celebration between Odysseus and Penelope the night before.

### Chapter 22: The Apple Of Discord

It was a time when there was a war such that the music of it has been heard across the centuries, from singer to singer and is likely to never cease.

The rivalries between men and gods have brought about a variety of catastrophes, but none as massive as this. the event would not happen as they claim were it taken place without jealousy between the immortals. All because of the golden apple! Yet Destiny has nurtured evil seedlings from the smallest of seeds This is the way in which one wickedness grew so large as to engulf earth and heaven.

The marine nymph thesis (whom Zeus himself had once wanted to be his wife) was married to a mortal Peleus Then there was a lavish wedding celebration at heaven. The immortals all were granted a wedding, except for Eris who was the goddess of Discord always a dreadful guests. However, she was not invited. As the guests of the wedding sat down to a the table, she stumbled on their laughter, dropped between them a golden apple then left with a look which suggested the worst. One of the guests picked up the odd missile and read its message"For the Fairest" soon, there was a lively discussion within the gods. The goddesses were all keen to win the prize but only three of them remained.

Venus, who is the beauty goddess, claimed that she was the one who had it her right. Juno did not want the idea of being less fair as a different person, and Athena was a fan of the hand of beauty, as well as of wisdom and could refuse to give it away! The discord was indeed at the wedding meal. The gods had not could have a chance to answer such the matter, and certainly at least not Zeus himself. Neither did the three competitors were forced to select a judge from among mortals.

In the past, at the foot of Mount Ida, near the city of Troy an unnamed young shepherd who was named of Paris. Paris was just as funny like Ganymede himself, the Trojan youngster that Zeus was in the form of an eagle took and carried away to Olympus in order to become an offering cup bearer to the gods. Paris also was an Trojan born royal and, however, just as Oedipus was placed on a mountain in his earliest years of life, since the Oracle predicted that he was to be the end of his family and ruin the country he was born into. Destiny helped and helped him to fulfil that prediction. He was raised as shepherd, and was responsible for his sheep on the mountains however, his beautiful appearance won the awe of those who were wooded and he also attracted the attention of the goddess Oenone.

At last the goddesses of three entrusted to him the judgement and golden apple. Juno was the first to stand before him in her splendor as the Queen of Gods and Men with her beloved peacocks who were beautiful to behold as her the royal fans.

"Use only the judgement of a prince Paris," she said, "and I will give to you wealth and royal power."

These majesties and assurances would have touched anyone's heart But the fervent Paris was required to listen to the arguments of competitors. Athena was standing in front of him, a sight as that was as warm and welcoming as the day, with her blue eyes, and golden locks under the golden headdress.

"Be mindful of me when you honor my name, Paris," she declared, "and I will give to you wisdom that lasts for ever, and great honor among the men and also acclaim during war."

Then, Venus shone upon him stunning as no one could imagine ever being. If she'd come without a name, like any other woman from the country, her beauty could have enthralled him as ocean-foam shining in the sun. But she was draped in her enchanting Cestus that enthralled him with the kind of beauty cannot be snuffed out by anyone.

With no bribes, she may be able to conquer the king, but she smirked at the man's dumb surprise, and said, "Paris, thou shalt be married to one of the prettiest women on earth."

In response the shepherd was elated and was able to kneel down and presented her with a golden apple. He did not pay attention to the goddesses who had been slighted. They disappeared in a storm which sounded like a the possibility of a storm.

In that time, was when he only sought advice of Venus while he merely wished for the road for his fortune. She informed him that his father was the king Priam of Troy And through her aid, he escaped the Nymph Oenone that he got married to, and set off in the search of his royal cousin.

It happened at the time that Priam announced a race of power between his sons as well as princes. He also offered as prize the most magnificent bull that was to be discovered in the herds of Mount Ida. The herdsmen came to pick, and as they snatched away the joy of Paris's heart, the prince continued through Troy with the thought of trying his luck and maybe win the prize back.

The events took place in front of Priam and Hecuba as well as their entire family and their children, which included the high-ranking princes Hector and Helenus as well as the young Cassandra and their daughter. A poor woman suffered a sad tale, regardless of her status as she was once in disdain for Apollo and was cursed to see the future as well as to see predictions discredited. In this particular day, only she was afflicted with bizarre fears.

However, if the man who was going to be the devastation of his country was to return to victory, he would have won. Paris took the title. In the moment of his celebration the poor Cassandra was able to see him through her visionary eyes. Seeing alongside all the guilt and suffering the man was about to inflict on her, she broke into tears and cried out in rage, and could have warned her fellow travelers of the dangers coming. However, the Trojans did not pay attention and were apt to regard her dreams as a shamanistic fable. Paris was back with them as a dazzling young woman as a winner; and when he told them the secrets of his birthplace, they turned the phrases of the Oracle into the wind, and embraced the shepherd as a lost prince.

So far, everything went well. However, Venus who's promise was not yet made, suggested that Paris find a vessel to search for the bride he was to marry. The prince was silent about the quest, but instead pleaded with his comrades to leave him; as well as circulating rumors about his search for the lost daughter of his father Hesione when he took off to Greece eventually settling in Sparta.

The prince was warmly welcomed by Menelaus King, as well as his wife, Fair Helen.

The queen was raised to be the child of Tyndarus and queen Leda however some believe they were the daughter of an enchanted swan and indeed, there was an enchanted aura around her. The greatest heroes from Greece have wooed her since she left the palace of her father to become the wife of King Menelaus as well as Tyndarus was afraid for her tranquility, bound her lovers to the oath. As per this promise that they would respect her choices, and help her husband in the event that they were to be taken away from her. Because in the entire world of Greece there was nothing as stunning as beautiful as Helen. Helen was one of the most beautiful women anywhere in the world.

So was Venus make good on her promises and the shepherd receive his prize with dishonor. Paris was a guest at the Court of Menelaus for a lengthy time as he was treated with courtly manner which he never returned. Because, when the king was during a trip to Crete His guest had gained the love of Fair Helen and convinced the princess to leave her husband and go to Troy.

King Menelaus returned with the empty nest of the Swan. Paris as well as the most beautiful woman of all had arrived safely across the Atlantic.

## Chapter 23: Heroes Of The Trojan War

The moment the deceit was exposed, the whole of Greece was ablaze with anger. They remembered their promise but wrath erupted on them for the injustice caused to Menelaus. They were, however, less angry over Fair Helen as they were with Paris as they were confident that the queen was attracted away from her homeland and from her perception by a spell of fascination. They sought advice on to figure out how they could bring Fair Helen to her home as well as her husband.

It had been a while from that reception when Eris was throwing the fruit of contention in the manner of a firebrand the guests. The ember of resentment that had burned for all the time exploded at last, and, fed by rivalries between men, and by the rivalries between the gods, it appeared as if it was igniting both earth and heaven.

The heroes responded to the call for arms unintentionally. The passage of time had brought them back to their loss to Fair Helen as well, and they resisted the urge to depart from their homes and comforts to fight, even in her defense.

One of them of them was Odysseus King of Ithaca and who was married to Penelope and was satisfied with his kingdom as well as his young son Telemachus. In fact, he was in awe of them, that he faked insaneness to avoid the wrath of his servants, and then seemed to have forgotten his connection with Penelope as he sloughed the shoreline and sowing salt into the sand in. However, a messenger named Palamedes who was sent with a summons to fight was sceptical that the abrupt rage could be an elaborate ploy, as the king was famous for being a master of numerous methods. Therefore, he stood there for a time (while Odysseus, pretending to not pay attention to his presence, was sloughing away in the sand) while he placed the baby Telemachus right into the path of the share in slough. The wise man's skills were not enough for him. Odysseus changed the slough in a sharp manner and snatched up the tiny prince and his fatherly senses had been revealed! Then he was unable to anymore play the as a madman. He was forced to leave of his wife Penelope and go on to become a part of the hero's team with no idea that he would not come back for another 20 years. After he was enlisted He set to serve the common cause of heroes and soon became the same ingenuity as Palamedes raising the spirits of lagged warriors.

The one remaining was to become the best warrior among all. It was Achilles who was the child of Thetis who was foretold in days of Prometheus as a person who would surpass his father in splendor and glory. The years had passed after the marriage of Thetis to Peleus, the King. Peleus and their child Achilles had grown into adulthood. He was a marvel of strength in itself in addition to being unaffected. His mother, who was warned of his demise during the Trojan War, had dipped into the sacred river Styx as just a baby to ensure that he would not be injury with any kind of weapon. From the head to the foot, she dipped him into and then forgot about the small heel she was holding his hand, which alone was a risk of being wounded in any way. However, even with all these precautions Thetis did not feel satisfied. In awe of the reports of war and coming, she was able to have her son carried up in a women's clothes, in the princesses of the King Lycomedes of Scyros to ensure that he could be able to escape notice from people and evade his fate.

In this palace it was Odysseus disguised as an merchant. He presented his goods to the royal family, including jewelry and ivory, exquisite fabric, as well as a variety of witty weapons. The queen's daughters wore the veils and girdles, as well as other items that women love However, Achilles who was unaware of similar things, pulled out the weapons and took them in the same fervor that showed his personality was exposed. He, too, accepted his fate and set off to join the heroics.

In every town, people were gathered together to build the ships as well as collecting supplies. The forces of the allied nations from Greece (the Achaeans, as they were known) picked Agamemnon as their chief of staff. He was a formidable man, and king of Mycenae and Argos and was the king's cousin of the wronged Menelaus. In second place to Achilles in power was the gigantic Ajax following him

Diomedes and then the smart Odysseus And Nestor was held with great respect due to his longevity and acclaim. They were the main heroes. Two years after intensive preparations, they arrived at their destination in Aulis and were ready to set sail towards Troy.

The delay in the beginning held them. Agamemnon has had the chance to kill a stag that was considered sacred to Diana The troops were stricken by plague and a calm prevented the vessels from being imprisoned. In the end, the Oracle revealed the cause for this calamity and demanded atonement for the young Iphigenia the daughter of Agamemnon's father. Amid a sigh of despair, the king accepted to sacrifice her as a kind of victim. the girl was prepared to be sacrificed. At the very last second Diana was able to take her in a fog and left an unmarked hind home, before bringing the girl into Tauris in Scythia and there she served as a priestess within the temple. While there, in the meanwhile time her friends and family members, in awe of the reason for her disappearance they mourned her dead. However, Diana was adamant about accepting their baby to be an offering and peace was brought to the troops with the blowing of the wind once more. Thus, the ships took off.

In Troy at sea in the sea, the elderly Priam and Hecuba provided shelter for their son Paris and his thieving wedding ring. There were some doubts about these guests however they prepared to protect their family and their citadel.

There were many greats in the Trojans and their allies. They were courageous and honest men whom it was not their fault that this disrepute should be imposed on them due to the culpability of the Prince Paris. They included Aeneas as well as

Deiphobus, Glaucus and Sarpedon and Priam's opulent son Hector who was the most powerful of his troops and the most important bulwark in Troy. The other heroes had a bitter regret for the moment that had taken Paris back to the city he had called home. However, he was able to stay in the company of his people and Trojans were forced to defend their cause against the hostile fleet which was swarming across the sea.

Even the gods sided with. Juno and Athena were the only gods who never forgotten the wrath of Paris at all, condemned Troy along with him, and supported the Greeks in addition to Poseidon God of sea. However, Venus was true to her beloved, defended her cause for the Trojans through all of her strength and convinced the war-like Mars to join in.

**Chapter 24: The Wooden Horse**

Over the course of nine years, Greeks took over Troy for nine years, and Troy was able to stand up against all devices. Both sides saw the lives of countless heroes were lost and the Greeks were forced to recognize the other as enemies of great courage.

The chief warriors would sometimes fight at single-handedly, while their armies watched and the old people of Troy along with women were seen watching away from the city's walls. The King Priam as well as Queen Hecuba were often there, as was Cassandra who was sad at the knowledge of their fate, as well as Andromache her beautiful young bride of Hector along with her small child, whom they called The City King. There were times when Fair Helen would look at the plain and the countrymen she'd abandoned even though she had been the reason for all of this conflict however, the Trojans partially repaid her for their sins when they passed, as her beauty seemed like an enchanting spell and she warm hearts like the sunlight mellows the apples. For nine years, the Greeks took over the towns around them however, the city of Troy did not let up, while the Grecian ships stood by in awe with their wings folded.

The other half can't be recorded this time, but during the tenth year in the war, many events were realized and the close of the war was close. In the tenth year in particular it is full of stories. The Greeks began to fight among their own over the scavengings from war. The great Achilles fled the army in anger and decided to not fight. He was unable to convince Achilles to return until his companion Patroclus was killed by the prince Hector. In the wake of that tragic news, Achilles rose in great force and returned to the Greeks after which he set out in the armor that was made to his specifications by Vulcan and the prayer of Thetis. In the vicinity of the River Scamander close to Troy He was confronted by and killed Hector after which he carried the body of his hero on his vehicle through the open plain. What happened when the old Priam wandered off by himself at evening to the camp of Achilles to extort the body of his son and then the way Achilles agreed to it, and also offered a truce in exchange for burial honors given to his enemies These things were so opulently sang that they are unable to be properly sung.

Hector The bulwark of Troy was slain and the destruction of Troy was close near. Achilles himself was not able to out his victory and as brutal in his actions, had no right to be punished for the manner in which he met his dying. The ruthless king was killed by Paris who never thought of pursuing him on the field. Paris although he created all this tragedy on Troy and put the risk on his fellow citizens. However, he waited for Achilles at a sacred temple to Apollo as well as from his hideout he shot an arrow that was poisoned at Achilles, the Hero. It struck his ankle, and the water from the Styx was not enough to awe the wound, and due to the venom, the great Achilles passed away. Paris was also killed shortly after through another arrow poisoned, however, that wasn't a long grieving for anybody!

But Troy was able to hold out and the Greeks that were unable resist it with force, considered the best way to capture the city by sleight of hand. In the end, with assistance from Odysseus they came up with an idea.

Some of the Grecian group broke group and set off like they were headed home;

however, after they were out of sight, the ships were anchored in the vicinity of an island. The remainder of the troops was then able to build the most beautiful representation of horses. They constructed it from wood, then fitted and carved along with a door carefully concealed so that nobody could ever see it. After the construction was completed it looked as an impressive idol. However, it was hollow, expertly punctured from time to time, and was so big that even a group of soldiers were able to hide within it and not be in danger. In this hideout went Odysseus, Menelaus, and the chiefs of the other tribes. They were fully equipped, and after the doors were shut on the trio, the remainder of the Grecian force broke camp and left.

In Troy there was a crowd of people who saw the departure of ships and word of it had become a blaze of news. The enemy of the great had lost hope after more than ten years of war! The army was been taken away; the remainder were moving. The last ships was sailing and the camp was empty. Tents that been whitening the land had vanished as a snowflake prior to the setting sunset. The battle was ended!

The entire town was filled over happiness. Much like one who was in prison for a long time and slammed the door open, the city broke free of all restrictions, and all stood as one to try the new liberty. liberation. The gates were opened and Trojans both women and men and kids poured over the open plains and into the dugout of the adversaries. They were greeted by in the middle was the Wooden Horse.

Nobody was aware of what the horse could have been. At first they were scared, but then the crowds gathered around it like children gathered in a horse's stall and marvelled at the incredible height and size and wished to move it to the city for the prize of battle.

In response, a man spoke, Laocoon, a priest of Poseidon. "Take heed, citizens," said he. "Beware of anything that is derived directly from Greeks. Are you fighting the Greeks for ten years, but not learned their strategies? It's a bit of deceit."

There was a second protest from the crowd and then a group members of the Trojans brought forward a miserable man wearing the clothing typical of an Greek. It appeared that he was the only surviving member from the Grecian army which is why they voted to save his life in the event that he told them the truth.

Sinon as that was the name used by the spy Sinon, claimed to have lost his way due to the evil of Odysseus And he informed his followers that Greeks constructed the Wooden Horse as an offering to Athena as a tribute to Athena, and constructed it as massive to prevent the horse from being taken from the camp because it was to be a triumphant sign for its owners.

The excitement of the Trojans increased and they began to use their mind to discover the fastest way to bring the horse across the plains and then into the city for victory. In the midst of their discussions the two enormous serpents arose from the ocean and flew toward the camp. The people who were there fled, and some were awestruck however, everyone, both near as well as far away, were watching the new sign of the times. With their heads up as the sea-serpents swam across the beach, fast and shining. They were as terrifying in the form of a rising flood that is descending on an utterly helpless town. Through the crowd, they were swept and grabbed the priest Laocoon in the place where he was along with his sons and wrapped them around and around in a terrifying coil. It was impossible to getting out. The father and the sons both perished as the creatures have devoured three of them and tossed them into the ocean, they fell back, removing all trace of the terror.

The scared Trojans believed that there was a signification for the situation. In their mind, a the punishment was coming to Laocoon because of his words about The Wooden Horse. It was surely holy to gods. the man had committed blasphemy and was dead in front of their the eyes of their. The villagers tossed his message at the wind. They decorated the horse's back with garlands and received praise; and finally with all hands on deck and dragging it slowly away from the camp to Troy. Troy. After the conclusion of their victory day they put aside all memories of fear and made fun in the midst of a decade of hardship.

It was at night when Sinon the spy slid open the door that was hidden in the Wooden Horse, and in the darkness Odysseus, Menelaus, and the other chiefs that had been hiding there, escaped and signaled that Grecian army. Because, in the darkness of darkness, the ships who were moored in the back of the island were sailing back to the mainland, and now the Greeks had landed in Troy.

There was no way that an ounce of Trojan was in the area of guard. The entire city was in celebration when the enemy appeared within its ranks and the threat of Laocoon was realized.

Priam and his men fell to the sword and the kingdom was robbed of its treasures as well as children and women's the treasure.

And lastly the city was destroyed to its base.

Homeward set sail for the Greeks and took as their royal prisoners poor Cassandra and Andromache as well as many other Trojan. Finally, home was Fair Helen and the root of all the sorrow determined to be forgiven by her husband King Menelaus. Because she was awakened by the magic of Venus as well as before the end of Paris she'd secretly been longing for home and a companion. The home of Sparta she travelled together with the King after an extremely stormy and long journey in which she lived and passed away the most beautiful of all women.

### Chapter 25: The God Of War

Ares God of battle and war He was the god of war and battle, who cared about virtually nothing else. He was the god of war and battle. Greeks believed that other gods defended them or aided them in beneficial ways and therefore they adored them. The only aid they would ever receive from Ares was what the god could provide them during the point of war. Even then, there was a chance that he would end up on the wrong side. Instead of being awed by him, as did Zeus as well as Apollo and Athena and Athena, they hated his name and referred to him as "bloody Ares," and "raging Ares," because of his rage. While they revered his gods, they did not intend to build as numerous temples to honor him just like the other gods.

There is nothing that Ares more than a war between two powerful armies. He loved watching the leaders speeding up towards one another in their war chariots. They had helmets on their heads as well as shields strapped to their arms. He enjoyed watching people throw spears and arrows shoot, and then strike their swords to each other. The noise and chaos of battles were a delight for him. The greater the number of people killed, the more he enjoyed the scene. Actually, Ares was so fond of fighting that he frequently came to earth from the heavens to take part in battles between soldiers. And then the bravest and strongest of warriors needed to make their way to Ares. However, even though gods were fond of fighting, he did not as successful in the same way as goddess Athena Her intelligence and cleverness to assist her during her struggles and Ares didn't stop to consider as he went on.

One time during the course of a major war, Ares was fighting against the Greeks as they drove everyone else before his. As Athena was aware of the situation, she came to aid them, as she believed that they'd taken the right side in the dispute that started the war and was not happy to see the Greeks defeated. If Ares was able to see her on the Greek flank in all her armor, he ran towards her, throwing his devastating spear into her breast. Athena took the spear's tip against her shield, then put it away. She then grabbed a huge stone, and shot towards Ares. The aim she chose was so certain that she struck him hard before he was thrown flat onto his back. He was a massive man that it was claimed that his body was 7 acres while he lay in the dirt. Ares was injured so badly by the blow that he resigned himself to his fight and ran away towards Mount Olympus. In the end, the Greeks and the aid of Athena gained victory.

The Greeks were fond of telling a account of how they believed Ares was a prisoner for a time. A long time ago according to them, two children were born and were christened Otus or Ephialtes. In the beginning, they were tiny and fragile, however they increased in size so quickly that they awed everyone with their beauty and size. As young as 9 years of age, they'd transformed into massive kings that stood over a hundred feet and were just equally brave and enormous. These giants are now farmers and they cherished the opportunity to be peaceful, and take care of their crops that were growing. However, Ares caused such continual warfare among people that the crops of their farmers were frequently lost as well as their fields wiped empty.

www.ingramcontent.com/pod-product-compliance
Lightning Source LLC
Chambersburg PA
CBHW071448080526
44587CB00014B/2030